Social Pedagogy in Child Education

Katherine Myrestad

Published by Katherine Myrestad, 2023.

While every precaution has been taken in the preparation of this book, the publisher assumes no responsibility for errors or omissions, or for damages resulting from the use of the information contained herein.

SOCIAL PEDAGOGY IN CHILD EDUCATION

First edition. November 6, 2023.

Copyright © 2023 Katherine Myrestad.

ISBN: 979-8223557906

Written by Katherine Myrestad.

For my family, my steadfast pillars of strength and encouragement. Your faith in me is the wind beneath my wings, and your love is the light guiding me through every word I write. You are my cheerleaders, the echo of my laughter, and the comfort in moments of doubt. Thank you for being my inspiration, my haven, and my heart's chorus.

Prologue

———

IN THE QUEST TO UNLOCK the vast potential within every child, educators turn to the timeless art and evolving science of pedagogy. "Social Pedagogy and the Art of Educating Children" is an academic foray into the myriad methods that have shaped the modern classroom. Within these pages lies a detailed exploration of pedagogical theories and practices, each thread woven into the fabric of educational philosophy. It is a collection of academic articles that I put together as an educational tool for our teachers, parents, pedagogues, school employees, child caregivers, and childcarers.

This book is a journey through the heart of teaching. It examines the roots of various pedagogical approaches, from the traditional to the transformative, and scrutinizes their application in the ever-changing tapestry of the classroom. Our voyage traverses the landscapes of cooperative learning, dives into the wellsprings of emotional intelligence, and scales the summits of critical thinking.

As we delve into the studies and statistics, the case studies and narratives, we keep the child firmly at the center of our discourse. For it is in the eyes of a child that the future of education is reflected, and it is through the wisdom of social pedagogy that we can guide them toward a horizon brimming with possibilities.

Let this book serve as a beacon for education, a scholarly compass pointing towards the confluence of care, learning, and development. As we turn each page, may we be inspired to mold our practices not only with the mind but with the heart, understanding that the art of educating children is, at its core, a social endeavor—a dance of knowledge and empathy.

Welcome to a scholarly exploration of what it means to educate, to grow, and to inspire—the very art of social pedagogy.

A Personal Journey from Survival to Child Advocacy

There's a saying that goes, "In every crisis, there is an opportunity." As cliché as it sounds, it held true for me when the crisis I faced became the opportunity that defined my life's path to where I am today — a resilient advocate, a bridge-builder, and a social pedagogue.

In my darkest hours, it was my son who shed light on our shared struggle. There was a time when my world was dominated by fear, living in an unstable, threatening environment with the biological father of my infant son. His escalating aggression filled our days with dread and uncertainty, putting us at risk. I was petrified that we could become another heartbreaking headline, another story of a mother and child lost to violence. This harrowing experience was our reality when my son was only a month old.

The fear that encircled us was a deafening alarm, and I knew I had to seek help. This pivotal decision introduced me to the lifeline that was social services — an entity that I was entirely grateful for. They offered us a haven, a protective shelter where we could breathe without fear. To further ensure our safety, we were moved to another part of the country, away from the storm that was in my past.

The experience was overwhelming, and yet, the people from the social services made it bearable. They guided us and provided the support we desperately needed. It was during this journey I saw the silver lining in my turmoil. The heroic efforts of the social workers ignited a spark in me, a drive to give back, to become a social pedagogue, and to support and make a difference in the lives of others who might be walking in my old shoes.

As I rebuilt my life, I saw my son flourish in a peaceful environment, a stark contrast to the first couple of months of his life. This, coupled with my own healing, solidified my resolve to ensure no child has to live in fear or uncertainty. As a social pedagogue, I am committed to building bridges between the school, parents, and social services to protect and nurture children's well-being.

Through my social pedagogy education, I learned the intricacies of social services — understanding its laws and regulations, and acknowledging its importance in our profession. As we dive deeper into these topics, I invite you to reflect on the protection of our children and the critical role we play in their lives. Why is it that, despite our best efforts, some children still live in horrific conditions, their safety compromised?

My personal journey of survival to advocacy is proof that with the right support and tenacity, we can turn our lives around. And that's what I wish to extend to every child I will be entrusted with — a chance for a better, safer life. With the knowledge of social services laws and regulations, we can effectively safeguard our children's rights, acting proactively to prevent any harm.

Yet, despite our collective efforts, we still find children being let down, their rights compromised, and living in unbearable situations. A change in a child's behavior could be a distress signal, requiring immediate attention and action. This begs the question — why are children still at risk? Why are they enduring harsh conditions despite systems in place to protect them?

Reflecting on these questions is crucial in our role as protectors of children's welfare. We must stay vigilant, acknowledge the warning signs, and act timely to avert any potential risks. After all, safeguarding children is not just a responsibility; it's our moral duty.

My journey from a fearful past to a hopeful future serves as a testament that with the right support, resilience, and unwavering spirit, one can overcome the hardest of circumstances. This understanding is what drives me to ensure that every child I work with gets a chance to lead a better, safer life, far from the fears and insecurities that I once knew. Together, we can make a difference. And we will.

A Story from the Heart and The Transformative Power of Social Pedagogy

I want to take a moment to introduce myself and share the journey I embarked upon in my life as a Social Pedagogue in Sweden. It's a heartfelt story of bridging the gap between formal education and the community, of creating a sustainable society through the principles of social pedagogy.

The concept of school as a central and important place in society, where more than just pedagogical activities should occur, is not new. Way back in 1956, in the Söderhamns Tidning (Kungliga Biblioteket, u.d.), the concept of "the school in the middle of the village" was discussed. This idea of the school being a conduit between home and society, of creating a space for community and activity, has persisted even today. It is a place that fosters a sense of belonging, develops relationships, and encourages both intellectual and social growth. It creates conditions to make the school an arena that can be effectively utilized by everyone in the vicinity. The concept of "School as an Arena" is a political initiative part of a long-term, systematic work to level the living conditions for the inhabitants of many cities in Sweden, including my home city.

It is this concept that I have incorporated into my classrooms. As a social pedagogue, I focus on the reciprocal interactions between individuals and society. Our theoretical roots are in philosophy, psychology, sociology, and pedagogy, giving us the capacity to understand and promote knowledge from the individual's inner workings to societal structures. But the crux of our work lies in turning this knowledge into actions.

The primary objectives of the "School as an Arena" initiative are manifold. They aim to increase the chances of student success, provide children with meaningful leisure time, create participation, and strengthen networks and contexts for adults around children. But how does this happen?

The answer lies in engagement and mobilization. Encouraging organizations and people in the school's vicinity to initiate various activities at and around the school is the way forward. But getting people to want to be part of communities that they or others have initiated is a challenge that we as social pedagogues need to know of.

Moreover, community involvement varies based on what is happening in society, where we are, and what is happening in our lives. An SCB survey showed that 2.4 million of Sweden's inhabitants are active in at least one association activity. These people choose to engage for various reasons, such as guilt, duty, life changes, or the desire to have a concrete impact, support others, or positively influence society.

Despite such extensive volunteer engagement, it is insufficient for all children to have equal opportunities to succeed in school, feel safe, and have meaningful leisure time. This is where social pedagogues come in. We work cross-sectorally to create conditions that collectively strengthen the compensatory mission of the school and create more equal growing conditions. This work is not just about treating the symptoms of societal problems; it's about addressing the root causes.

In conclusion, as a social pedagogue and educator, I aim to engage and mobilize communities, foster inclusivity, and bridge the gap between school and society. It's about fostering a transformative process that allows individuals, groups, and society to change, dare, and want to change. Social pedagogy is more than just a profession for me; it's a vocation, a calling that empowers me to make a real difference in the world, one student and one community at a time.

Remember, dear readers, change begins with one person, and one action, and it often starts with education. Let us continue to foster an environment of growth, inclusivity, and sustainability in our classrooms and beyond. Thank you for allowing me to share my journey with you today, and I hope it inspires you to make a difference in your way.

From Social Pedagogue to Spiritual Coach: My Evolution as a Modern Woman

In the myriad complexities of the modern world, every woman charts her unique path. My journey is a tapestry of diverse roles — social pedagogue, mentor, author, spiritual coach, and mother. Each role and each interaction has shaped me, and in return, I've had the honor of shaping lives and making a difference.

As a social pedagogue, I've tutored five children, creating individualized support strategies to help each child excel academically. With a heart full of compassion and a mind brimming with techniques to engage them, we collectively achieved a 20% increase in their average grades, paving their way to higher education. The spark in their eyes, their sincere gratitude, and the evident changes in their lives were affirmations of my purpose.

Simultaneously, I supported adolescents with neurodevelopmental disorders, guiding them toward an active and socially inclusive life. The job was challenging, yet deeply rewarding. Helping these individuals gain independence and a better quality of life taught me the incredible resilience of the human spirit.

However, my journey did not stop there. As I continued my education in social pedagogy, my role as a mentor evolved into becoming a spiritual coach. This path allowed me to delve deeper into the intangible dimensions of existence. The spiritual aspect became a compass guiding me through the labyrinth of life, aiding others, and discovering my inner peace.

My transformation seeped into my writings. As I began to share my insights on an online global platform, I discovered a community resonating with my experiences. My words — whether stories, poems, or personal anecdotes — reflected the essence of personal growth, motivation, and the shared human experience.

And then, there is motherhood. My children, especially my youngest, only six years old, are a constant source of inspiration. Every day, they teach me about innocence, wonder, and the power of unconditional love. Being a spiritual coach has enriched my relationship with them, allowing me to guide them with wisdom, compassion, and respect for their paths.

Looking back, my journey is a testament to personal evolution and the power of nurturing connections. Each child I guided, each adolescent I assisted, each reader who found solace in my words, and my children, all contribute to the woman I am today. My growth is intertwined with theirs, creating a continuous ripple effect.

In the words of Eleanor Roosevelt, "The purpose of life is to live it, to taste experience to the utmost, to reach out eagerly and without fear for newer and richer experiences." My experiences, filled with lessons, growth, and transformation, echo this sentiment. Life presents an opportunity not just to exist, but to evolve, share, and inspire. This is the essence of being a modern woman today.

As we navigate our journeys, remember that our stories are threads in the grand tapestry of womanhood. Embrace them, share them, and continue to thrive in your unique way.

The Art of Changing Lives, One Community at a Time

Have you ever wondered about the magic behind a thriving, interconnected community? As a social pedagogue, that's what I spend most of my days on. I am deeply committed to facilitating the growth of individuals within their communities. I've dedicated my career to exploring and applying social pedagogy principles in a myriad of settings.

Social pedagogy, for those unfamiliar with the term, is an approach that combines education and social work, focusing on holistic learning and development. It is a way of working with every individual's inherent potential. I have my roots in this practice and have developed my expertise through rigorous study and practice.

The Book

I have been particularly influenced by the book "Renässans för socialpedagogik? En bok om socialpedagogisk bildning" (Renaissance for social pedagogy? A book on social pedagogic education) by Elisabeth Cedersund, Lisbeth Eriksson, Bibbi Ringsby Jansson, and Lars A Svensson. This book explores the role of social pedagogy in both historical and contemporary contexts, stating the theoretical framework of social pedagogy is experiencing a renaissance, while also facing challenges, particularly from the growing influence of social work in European nations.

The authors take readers through a thorough theoretical and historical journey, connecting various knowledge bases such as philosophy, sociology, and pedagogy with social pedagogy. They illuminate the works of several key figures like Hannah Arendt, known for her social philosophical perspective on action and interaction, and John Dewey and Paolo Freire, who significantly impacted social pedagogy development, albeit in different ways.

The authors also offer glimpses of social pedagogic practices worldwide, including established "institutions" like Kominkan in Japan, Mahalla in Uzbekistan, and the Settlement Movement in the USA. These institutions represent local, social-pedagogically influenced communities that serve as tangible demonstrations of social pedagogy's potential impact.

Addressing Challenges

Renaissance for social pedagogy? A book on social pedagogic education does not skirt around the challenges in social pedagogy. It candidly addresses the growing influence of social work in European nations and how it could dilute the unique features of social pedagogy. The authors bring into sharp focus the complexities of power relations within social pedagogy — an issue that I encounter frequently in my work.

A Journey of Continual Learning

A recurring theme in the book is the importance of continual learning and adaptability in the field of social pedagogy. As our understanding of individuals and communities evolves, social pedagogy must adapt. This is a sentiment I strongly resonate with and strive to embody in my practice.

In essence, this book serves as more than just a teaching tool; it's a compass guiding my journey as a social pedagogue, continually challenging and shaping my understanding, practice, and perspective of this profound field.

Theory Meeting Practice

My practice as a social pedagogue is firmly grounded in these principles. I aim to build relationships based on mutual trust, reciprocal respect, and a common purpose. I believe in the transformative power of social pedagogy to affect individual and societal change.

However, like any practice, social pedagogy faces its own challenges. The book brings into sharp focus the complexities of relational power within the practice of social pedagogy. As a practitioner, I constantly grapple with these issues, working diligently to maintain equitable relationships within the community.

Social pedagogy, as a field, necessitates continuous learning and adaptability. The book suggests that prior knowledge in philosophy, sociology, and pedagogy can prove beneficial for readers, which aligns with my personal experience. As an ever-evolving student of social pedagogy, I have found that this interdisciplinary approach enriches my understanding and equips me better to serve my community.

Final thoughts

My journey as a social pedagogue isn't just about my personal growth; it's about the growth of my community. I constantly learn, adapt, and innovate my practice to meet the evolving needs of my community. Through this piece, I share a part of my journey and the wisdom that has shaped it, hoping to inspire more people to embrace the enriching field of social pedagogy. Together, we can leverage it as a tool to create a ripple of positive impact in our communities.

Revolutionizing Education Through Emotion and Empathy

In the often-stoic world of education, certain individuals stand out — those who are brave enough to revolutionize our perspective towards teaching and learning. One such figure is me, a social pedagogue hailing from Sweden. My profound vision and dedication toward a novel educational perspective resonate with those who yearn for a teaching environment that thrives on the joy of discovery, individuality, and personal interest.

The Vision: Emotion-Driven Education

My vision of pedagogy stands as a beacon, directing future teaching approaches. I strongly believe that learning should evoke joy and ignite curiosity, encouraging students to learn for their gratification and development. This belief is inspired by my personal experience; I was one of those students who experienced the joy of learning but often questioned the purpose behind the knowledge bestowed in school.

I could comprehend the names of all the rivers in Sweden or the cities of Europe, but it was not clear how this knowledge would help me grow as a person or contribute to society. While the school rewarded high scores and parents basked in the glory of good grades, the true value of knowledge remained a foreign concept.

The Transformation

I eventually broke free from this system, embracing my role as an outsider. As a form of rebellion, I started questioning the significance of the knowledge forced upon me. The education system failed to recognize me for who I was, focusing instead on my academic achievements. Fortunately, a single beacon of hope, a teacher, her name was Catherine. She acknowledged my individuality, treating me as a human rather than a problem.

She asked me what I thought and how I felt, giving me an unprecedented sense of being seen and valued. This was my first encounter with meaningful learning — when my entire existence was incorporated into the learning process. Catherine, with her seemingly insignificant acts, left a lasting impression on my life. Her influence introduced me to the essence of respect and consideration for the individual in the learning process, providing me with a new perspective on education.

The Revelation: Meaningful Learning

As a part of my Social Pedagogue education, I attended a thought-provoking lecture titled "Teaching and Meaningful Learning". The lecture emphasized the importance of knowledge's qualitative aspect — its ability to create meaning for the learner. This process entails relating the teaching material to prior understanding, placing new knowledge into context, and leading to a profound understanding that transforms one's perception of the world.

Throughout my training, this concept of meaningful teaching became a constant companion. It inspired me to explore deeper and to seek a comprehensive understanding that would allow me to incorporate this perspective into my work methods.

The Pedagogical Approach: An Emphasis on the Individual

In my pursuit of redefining pedagogy, I believe that students must be given opportunities to discover the context and function of the teaching material independently. This encourages them to form a personal relationship with the new information. As an educator, my role transforms into a guide, assisting students to take responsibility for their learning. This not only gives students a sense of ownership over their education but also answers the question — why should I learn this?

Encouraging students to believe in their thoughts and ideas, providing positive feedback, reinforcing their strong points, and understanding their worldview are all crucial elements of your teaching philosophy. According to researcher Madsén, having faith in one's abilities is a fundamental prerequisite for learning. This attitude enables meaningful interaction between students' everyday concepts and the subject's theories and concepts.

I maintain that the learning situation should be a creative process where the learner actively approaches new information by questioning it. A continuous critical approach toward the content helps the learner process new information in a personalized way.

Final thoughts

My journey into social pedagogy presents a clear message — learning should be an active, mental process leading to new experiences and insights. Using new knowledge to draw new conclusions or to act on new insights is the lifeline of meaningful knowledge. And it is this revolutionary approach to education that makes a true game-changer in the world of social pedagogy.

The Gap Between Theory and Practice in the Classroom

My experience has been enhanced through studies and real-life practice, which has indeed broadened my understanding of the complex world of social pedagogy. This path led me to one of the pivotal books of this discipline: "De fem stora" by Jesper Ersgård, which enlightens readers about five important aspects of education, shedding light on how we can significantly impact a student's learning journey.

Paradigm Shift: The Transition from Knowing to Doing

Our journey begins with understanding the fundamental paradigm shift that occurred in Sweden's education system in 1994. This shift, as described by Ersgård, pivoted the focus of our educational framework from "what a student knows" to "what a student does with what they know." This transformed teachers into guides, assisting students to apply knowledge rather than merely retaining information. While this fostered the development of complex abilities, it also came with challenges, leaving many students feeling lost in their skills development journey. A pedagogue's role here is to empower and guide these students toward self-assured capability and independence.

The Role of the Teacher and The School System

Understanding the school system's role in this paradigm shift is paramount. Michel Fullan, an esteemed education researcher, delineates four significant steps for school development. At the heart of these steps lies the establishment of trust and collaboration among teachers, making the teaching process more cooperative and effective. For Fullan, an evidence-based approach is essential, helping educators understand what works best in classrooms, creating a nurturing environment for students, and building an effective teaching framework. In this context, teachers aren't just pedagogues; they become key agents of change and development in the educational system.

Making Teaching Effective: The Impact of John Hattie

John Hattie, an education researcher known for his work on teaching effectiveness, suggests that we need evidence for what works in education. He identified various factors influencing a student's learning, categorizing them into six areas — the student, the home, the school, the teacher, the curriculum/development program, and the teaching method. For Hattie, the most effective influence on learning comes from the teacher, underlining the teacher's significance in shaping a student's learning journey.

The Power of Collaboration: Insights from Helen Timperley

One crucial part of the teaching process is the constant development of teachers themselves, as championed by Helen Timperley. She underscores that all professional development should ultimately lead to increased student learning. The goal is to foster a culture of shared, collegial learning that leads to more effective teaching, driven by students' learning needs, not solely the visions of the school management. This approach promotes results-oriented education, focusing on the impact of teaching methods on students, rather than the methods themselves.

Enhancing Learning: Dylan William's Perspective

Dylan William presents five crucial strategies for effective teaching, emphasizing the importance of clear objectives, a supportive classroom environment, feedback, peer response, and self-assessment. For William, feedback doesn't necessarily lead to learning; it's how students perceive and react to the feedback that truly matters. He also highlights the importance of a safe and secure classroom environment where it's okay to make mistakes, thus promoting better learning outcomes.

Understanding Mindset: The Work of Carol Dweck

Finally, we must touch on Carol Dweck's work on mindset. She explains how a person's belief about their abilities significantly affects their learning. She divides learners into those with a fixed mindset, who believe their intelligence is static, and those with a growth mindset, who see intelligence as something that can be developed. As educators, recognizing these mindsets and fostering a growth mindset is paramount for a student's learning journey.

Throughout my journey as a Social Pedagogue, the diverse perspectives and theories I encountered offered an enriched understanding of the intricate world of education. They empowered me to become a catalyst for change, ensuring that each student I interact with realizes their potential. This journey isn't easy, but it's incredibly rewarding.

To all my fellow educators out there, remember — every day in the classroom is a chance to change lives, to empower our students to grow, learn, and embrace their potential. Every step we take in this journey can indeed make a significant impact on the students' lives.

In closing, I'd like to share one of my favorite quotes from Carol Dweck: "Effort is one of the things that gives meaning to life. Effort means you care about something, that something is important to you and you are willing to work for it."

To the resilient educators, let's continue striving and thriving in our mission.

Embracing Non-Traditional Roles As a Woman and Mother

I feel compelled to share with you some very personal reflections about societal norms, especially those associated with gender. Stereotypes about how men and women should behave are embedded in our society, forming what we refer to as 'male norms' and 'female norms'.

As a mother of three boys, my home has been brimming with testosterone. My eldest two have grown into passionate football players, while my middle son voluntarily served in the Swedish Home Guard, eventually becoming a group leader.

Growing up, they adhered, quite unconsciously, to the male norms around them. They teased each other to grow stronger, worked hard on their fitness, and rarely complained about anything. All of this seemed to be part of being a boy, or rather, being a man.

But as I read up on gender norms, I realized something profound: I, too, was caught up in the 'male norm'. As the primary role model for my sons, my behavior reflected the stereotypical male strength and resilience.

I have been a single mother since they were very young. Having immigrated with my parents and children to a new country, I never stopped fighting for my family's well-being and prosperity. My sons see me as the strongest person they know, often praising me for being brave, strong, and capable.

However, I now see things from a different perspective.

Society deems the norm to be married or cohabitating, to live in your homeland, and to have an education by the time you're 40. At 46, I realize that I don't fit into these norms — and I'm quite content with that.

Despite the odds, I believe that my family and I have succeeded. And we are happy. To me, that's what matters the most.

What surprised me in the video clip I watched was how easily we accept various stereotypes or prejudices as norms. For instance, phrases like 'plays like an old woman', or the expectation of men to hide their softer, more vulnerable side.

I, too, have always tried to hide my vulnerabilities in front of my sons, believing that they needed a strong figure to look up to, especially since they lacked the presence of a father — another societal norm.

However, acknowledging the privileges we enjoy in society is crucial.

To develop as a person and professional, to serve a function in society, to have the opportunity to work and own a home, to access healthcare, to be seen, to be a fully functioning individual in society, and to educate oneself regardless of age, gender, or background — these are privileges often overlooked.

By acknowledging and addressing these societal norms, I hope we can foster a society where gender doesn't dictate expectations, allowing each one of us to create our unique paths.

Embracing the Challenges on a Journey Through Autism and ADHD

From the moment I first read the book 'Autism and ADHD in school' by David Edfelt, Annelie Karlsson, Ann Lindgren, and Anna Sjölund, I knew that I had found a guide that would profoundly influence my journey as a Social Pedagogue. My encounter with the book wasn't coincidental. It was a thoughtful gift, marking the beginning of a transformative experience that would later shape my approach to Social Pedagogy.

Understanding Autism and ADHD

One of the first lessons the book offers is a comprehensive understanding of autism and ADHD. It covers the practical consequences of having a weak central coherence, unusual perception, and poor Theory of Mind, and the impact of these on working memory and time perception. Such nuances in understanding the conditions are vital because they help avoid the common mistake of attributing the struggles of those living with autism or ADHD to laziness. For instance, a weak working memory can lead to forgetfulness, often misinterpreted as negligence or carelessness.

Creating Motivation for Children with Autism and ADHD

One of the key takeaways from the book is the importance of well-being for learning, a concept I've seen validated through Martin Seligman's research. As a social pedagogue, I firmly believe that creating a conducive environment based on individual needs and abilities is fundamental. Having experienced periods of depression during my schooling years, I relate deeply to the struggle students face when their environment is not tailored to their needs.

TEACCH: A Visual Approach to Pedagogy

The TEACCH method, an educational approach developed in the United States, has had a profound impact on my work. The authors of the book also advocate for a visually enhancing pedagogical method specifically designed for students with autism. While research on visual support for students with ADHD is limited, evidence suggests that visual reminder support can be beneficial. Nevertheless, understanding that not all students are visually inclined is crucial. Some students, including myself, prefer conventional text over visuals.

Drawing From Personal Experiences

The personal experiences I've had and the lessons I've learned have significantly shaped my work. The awareness of my own struggles with group interactions, for instance, led to an understanding that processing information in group settings can be overwhelming for some, myself included. This insight opened up a new perspective on how certain difficulties aren't just imagined but are the result of dealing with too many details simultaneously.

The Impact

The book 'Autism and ADHD in school' has been instrumental in my journey as a social pedagogue. It has not only provided me with invaluable insights into the diagnosis and impact of autism and ADHD, but it has also offered practical solutions that I've integrated into my work. I highly recommend it to all parents with children with NPF diagnoses and all school personnel.

Final Thoughts

In the world of social pedagogy, having a theoretical understanding is crucial. Still, the ability to translate that theory into real-world application is what truly makes the difference. As I continue my journey, I aim to further blend my personal experiences, theoretical knowledge, and practical work, sharing my findings with those who can benefit from them.

A Dive into Pedagogical Philosophies

Education is an evolving field that is shaped by philosophical and pedagogical theories, forming the basis of our understanding of knowledge and learning. As an invested social pedagogue, I have dedicated time to explore these foundational theories, which I'd like to share with you. My journey to understand knowledge and learning has led me to philosophers like Plato, Aristotle, and John Dewey, as well as pedagogues like Lev Vygotsky. The insights gleaned from their works are instrumental in shaping contemporary education.

The Classics

Let's start with our classical Greek philosophers. Plato, one of the most prominent figures in Western philosophy, suggested that knowledge could be attained through intellectual stimuli. His philosophical stance, known as rationalism, posited that by analyzing the world and thinking logically, we could unlock knowledge.

In contrast, Aristotle, Plato's illustrious student, believed that learning is best achieved through physical work and putting ideas into practice, a perspective known as empiricism. According to him, knowledge is gained through experience.

In the modern era

In the modern era, John Dewey, a proponent of pragmatism, argued that education should emphasize the development of abilities over the mere accumulation of facts. He believed that education should prepare individuals to participate actively in society by promoting their ability to acquire, scrutinize, and assess information. Dewey's ideas, including his assertion that theory and practice should be closely linked, have had a significant influence on the education system in countries like Sweden.

Yet another perspective is provided by Lev Vygotsky, who propagated the socio-cultural perspective. Vygotsky believed that knowledge is a social construction influenced by culture and best acquired through social communication. He argued that learning precedes development and emphasized the role of more knowledgeable individuals, such as teachers, in guiding learners.

The education system in our society

In the context of a society characterized by a high flow of information, the ability to sift, critically examine, and utilize knowledge is paramount. The school environment must adapt to changing societal conditions, like advancements in information technology, and focus on fostering abilities that allow students to independently acquire knowledge in contexts outside school.

To truly foster democratic citizens, our education system should bridge the gap between theory and practice, providing students with active tasks that build upon their experiences and relate to society at large. An approach centered on group work and problem formulation allows for the exchange of experiences and knowledge, while also providing students with opportunities to understand perspectives other than their own.

Final thoughts

The application of these philosophical and pedagogical theories in real-world contexts can bring about profound changes in our approach to learning and teaching. After all, the ultimate goal of education is not to merely impart knowledge, but to equip individuals with the skills and understanding needed to function and thrive in society.

Understanding different pedagogical perspectives is critical to enriching our learning environments and ensuring that our approach to education remains relevant in our rapidly changing world.

Balancing Knowledge and Child-Centered Approaches

As deeply engaged in norm-critical pedagogy, I consistently endeavor for a more inclusive and tolerant education system. My pedagogical stance, rooted in questioning and challenging ingrained norms and power structures, aims to create an inclusive and safe classroom environment that encourages open dialogue and respect for diversity. Moreover, as a mother of three boys, I strive to instill in them these norm-critical principles, nurturing their growth into conscientious and respectful individuals, who view the world from an inclusive perspective.

In my experience and observation, debates in education are often presented as a dichotomy: the traditional 'chalk-and-talk' approach emphasizing knowledge and discipline, versus a more child-centered approach that values children's interests, erroneously labeled as "knowledge-resistant." This polarized perspective, unfortunately, slots educators and stakeholders into one camp or the other, when, in reality, most would agree that a balanced pedagogical approach involves taking both the child and knowledge into account.

I propose we envision the child and knowledge as two poles amidst which pedagogical questions emerge. This perspective necessitates that we consider the quality of education in relation to both the learning process of children and the substance of the knowledge being taught. The currently polarized debate hinders any profound discourse on pedagogical and didactical issues. It's high time we challenged this oversimplified view and focused on creating a more nuanced educational discourse.

Constructivism as an educational theory

Constructivism, an educational theory emphasizing learners constructing their own understanding of the world, has become a dividing line between these two positions. Critics argue that constructivism can lead to an education that allows students too much freedom to explore the world on their own, thereby failing to give them access to the knowledge schools are tasked with teaching. This critique is important and provides an avenue for us to discuss whether constructivism overly emphasizes student exploration at the expense of acquiring knowledge.

However, it would be detrimental to disregard the principles of constructivist theories on learning and knowledge formation entirely. These theories have been, and still are, central to our understanding of how children can acquire knowledge.

Constructivist theories posit that knowledge imparted by teachers isn't directly copied into students' minds but rather reconstructed individually in interaction with learning materials and peers. Hence, the outcomes can be different for different students depending on their previous knowledge and abilities.

Key foundational elements in most constructivist theories are the theories of development and learning by Piaget and Vygotskij. For many years, Piaget's theory of cognitive development ruled, offering insights into the importance of understanding each student's preconditions for learning.

Socio-cultural changes in the context of constructivism theory

However, over the last three decades, Piaget's theory has been increasingly challenged by socio-cultural theories on learning and knowledge formation. These theories emphasize social dimensions in learning, leading to a shift from focusing on individual understanding to the context of learning and collective meaning-making. A prominent figure in this evolution is Vygotskij, with his theory on language and learning.

Unlike Piaget, who saw cognitive development as primary to knowledge development, Vygotskij emphasized the internalization of knowledge by the individual. He argued that social development precedes cognitive development. As Vygotskij famously said, cultural development in children is a two-step process, first between people and then inside the individual. According to him, an individual needs to be able to express understanding before individual meaning-making can develop.

One could argue that Piaget prioritized the child over knowledge, while Vygotskij prioritized knowledge over the child. Yet, these theories are not anti-knowledge or anti-child. They consider knowledge as a vital component and it's this knowledge that the individual moves towards. Both theories have inspired the development of pedagogical models and theories, but these models show a wide variation that can't be fully explained by the theories that inspired them.

It is not accurate to state that a specific pedagogy follows from these theories of learning and knowledge formation. Instead, they are useful for analyzing and understanding learning, or lack thereof, in various teaching situations. Piaget's main contribution is perhaps an understanding of cognitive preconditions and obstacles in students, while Vygotskij's main contribution is understanding different teaching contexts in terms of how they create conditions for students' internalization of knowledge.

Final thoughts

To make constructivism a dividing line in the school debate is unfortunate and could be devastating for the pedagogical discussion. As constructivist theories of learning and knowledge formation deal with the child-knowledge relationship, to dismiss them outright could harm the very thing that can bridge the false opposition created by reducing the question to the child or knowledge.

We need to ensure that neither the child nor knowledge is singularly central to our educational approach. Instead, the questions and problems that pique the children's interest and to which knowledge is a response should be at the heart of education.

A Personal Exploration on Montessori Pedagogy

In the heart of Italy, on August 31, 1870, a woman named Maria Montessori was born into a family of well-educated and successful middle-class parents. Right from the start, her strong will was evident, refusing to limit herself to the traditionally accepted professions for women of that time, such as teaching (Hainstock, 1999). Maria Montessori's trailblazing spirit enabled her to defy societal norms, and in 1896, she made history by becoming the first female doctor in Italy. It was this revolutionary spirit that led me down my own path as a social pedagogue, deeply influenced by her insightful methodology.

A Heart for the Unseen: Montessori's Early Contributions

Following her education, Montessori joined a research team studying children with mental disabilities, a demographic that was largely overlooked and marginalized during that era. These children were deprived of stimulation in their environment, an aspect that profoundly upset Maria. She dedicated her life to improving their conditions by studying the work of Frenchmen Jean Itard and Edouard Séguin, who specialized in helping children with mental disabilities (Skjöld Wennerström & Bröderman Smeds, 1997). They developed materials designed to stimulate and train different sensory functions, which later became integral to Montessori's revolutionary pedagogical approach.

With time, Montessori became the head of a school for mentally disabled children, where she refined and expanded on Itard and Séguin's ideas. The result was astounding, with the children exceeding expectations in their learning progress. This success led to the revolutionary idea of implementing the same teaching material for normal-gifted children, sowing the seed for the establishment of the Montessori method of education.

The Birth of Montessori Pedagogy

In 1907, Montessori was entrusted with the responsibility of running a daycare in a slum area in Rome, called Casa dei Bambini, or "House of Children." Here, she meticulously designed an environment that encouraged children to choose what they wanted to do and how long they wanted to do it. They were free to explore, but without disturbing each other, while being closely observed by Montessori herself. The astounding success of this preschool soon made headlines, leading to Montessori offering courses to train other teachers. In no time, her ideas spread across the world, and Montessori Pedagogy was born (Skjöld Wennerström & Bröderman Smeds, 1997).

Montessori's Philosophy: Following the Child

If I were to condense Montessori pedagogy into one sentence, it would be, "Follow the child" (Hedlund, 1995). This approach centers around each child's individual needs, putting the child's growth and development in focus. It emphasizes respecting a child's interests and activities, leveraging their unique learning abilities. The children are encouraged to learn using multiple senses and their entire body, thereby making their own experiences. This freedom of choice bolsters the effectiveness of learning, allowing them to explore activities either independently or in groups (Hainstock, 1999).

Another cornerstone of Montessori Pedagogy is the role of the educator. Montessori coined the term "directress" or "director" to better define this role, reflecting that the teacher's role is not to 'instruct' but to guide the child in their learning process (Hainstock, 1999). The educator is more of an observer, facilitator, and guide who creates an environment that promotes learning and is always prepared to assist the child when needed.

The educator's role is significant and multi-faceted, from preparing the environment to making it a stimulating learning space, from observing the child to offering necessary support and intervention, and from helping to build social relations to setting limits in a respectful way. The educator's ultimate goal is to help children become independent, responsible, and thoughtful individuals.

The Prepared Environment

One integral aspect of Montessori pedagogy is the carefully prepared environment, which includes an array of didactic material designed to help the child develop intellectually, emotionally, and physically. This setup respects a child's need to finish their chosen task without unnecessary interruption (Hainstock, 1999). This environment, devoid of strict schedules, gives the child the freedom to decide when they are done with a task and ready to move on to another. It's a classroom built to let the child move freely and choose where and with whom they want to work (Skjöld Wennerström & Bröderman Smeds, 1997).

Montessori Materials

The Montessori classroom's materials are designed to inspire continuous learning. They not only serve as a concrete aid to understanding but also prepare children for later learning stages. The Montessori materials are self-correcting to a large extent, which means they are designed so that the child can see their own mistakes and correct them, rather than being corrected by a teacher. This self-correction fosters a greater drive for learning and leads to what Montessori pedagogy calls "abstraction" (Skjöld Wennerström & Bröderman Smeds, 1997).

Critical Reflections on the Montessori Method

While Montessori Pedagogy offers a fundamentally different approach to education and has been globally recognized, it is not without its critiques. Some educators argue that the method lacks structure and traditional academic rigor. Moreover, critics point out that the emphasis on individual learning may limit the development of social skills (Malm, 2004).

However, supporters argue that these criticisms often stem from misunderstandings of the method. The freedom given to children in Montessori classrooms does not mean an absence of structure but a different kind of structure — one that respects the child's own rhythms and choices. Additionally, while the focus is on individual learning, cooperative learning, and socialization are integral to the Montessori classroom (Lillard, 2017).

My Montessori Journey: Transformation and Growth

As I reflect on my own journey embracing Montessori Pedagogy, I am filled with a sense of transformation and growth. The Montessori method not only influences the children I work with but also me as an educator. It has challenged me to rethink my role as a teacher and reimagine the classroom environment. The method pushes me to be more of a guide and less of a dictator, to listen more and speak less, and to observe more and interfere less.

Moreover, the Montessori approach has heightened my sensitivity to each child's unique capabilities, potential, and pace of learning. It has taught me to respect the individuality of each child, which in turn, has enabled me to tailor learning experiences that cater to their unique needs.

Montessori's philosophy goes beyond academics; it is about raising individuals who are empathetic, self-reliant, creative, and critical thinkers. It is about nurturing children who are not afraid to ask questions, make mistakes, learn, and grow. This has been the most rewarding aspect of my journey as a Montessori pedagogue — seeing children develop a lifelong love for learning and growing into responsible, caring, and independent individuals.

Final thoughts

Maria Montessori's visionary approach has indelibly marked the landscape of education, offering a refreshing perspective on child-centric learning. As a social pedagogue, the Montessori method continues to influence my professional journey, encouraging me to foster a learning environment that respects children's individuality and stimulates their inherent curiosity. The beauty of Montessori's philosophy lies in its simplicity, respect for the child's individuality, and the freedom it provides to learn at one's own pace.

Following in the footsteps of Maria Montessori, each one of us can aspire to revolutionize learning spaces, catalyze curiosity, and create a world where every child feels valued, heard, and inspired to learn.

How Rationalism, Empiricism, Pragmatism, and Socio-Cultural Perspectives Shape Our Understanding of Learning and Knowledge

The nature of knowledge and how learning can be conveyed or arise has long been a subject of discussion among philosophers and educators. Broadly, the lines have been drawn between rationalists and empiricists, those who believe that knowledge is best reached through theoretical thought experiments, and those who argue that knowledge is based on one's experiences. Famous philosophers like Plato and Aristotle debated how knowledge can and should be conveyed during antiquity.

Plato argued that knowledge is achieved through intellectual stimuli. Humans possess knowledge that can be drawn out through intellectual thought processes or through dialogues and discussions with others. This tradition is often referred to as rationalism, which suggests that knowledge can be achieved through a careful analysis of the world and through logical thinking. Rationalism sees learning as a matter of how people think.

Aristotle, on the other hand, argued that learning is achieved through physical work, by turning ideas into action and practical execution. In short, knowledge is gained through experience. This tradition is known as empiricism.

Pragmatism

The pragmatist and sociocultural perspectives have a more abstract view of knowledge than behaviorism and cognitivism. John Dewey's pragmatic perspective on learning has had a significant influence on education systems, including Sweden's. In a society with a vast flow of information, it's important for students not to just memorize and reproduce knowledge, but to be able to sift through, critically examine, and use knowledge. Education should be set in relation to the social and communicative context in which it takes place, i.e., society at large.

Dewey believed that the school should nurture students into democratic citizens, which includes equipping students to participate in society. To participate in a democratic society, every person needs to have the ability to absorb, scrutinize, and evaluate information. A problem, according to Dewey, arises when there is a gap between theory and practice, which is common in a teaching situation. The task of the school is to bridge the gap through student-active tasks based on students' experiences related to society at large.

The sociocultural perspective

The sociocultural perspective on learning originates primarily from Lev Vygotsky's work. Vygotsky was an educator who lived and worked in the Soviet Union in the 1920s and 30s. Like Dewey, Vygotsky emphasized student-active methods and opposed ideas that are characteristic of behaviorism. Vygotsky believed that knowledge is a social construct influenced by culture and is best assimilated through social communication, i.e., between individuals in interaction.

Criticism of Vygotsky's theories and the sociocultural perspective has been hard to find in literature. A potential critique of the sociocultural perspective could be its relevance to learning and assessment in schools. The sociocultural perspective complicates the construction and assessment of examinations as individual tests are conducted without the possibility of social interaction. An assessment process according to sociocultural theory would mainly advocate collective examinations, which cannot always be conducted in Swedish schools where students ultimately have to be assessed individually and on an individual basis.

Social pedagogy

It is an approach that combines education and social work to provide holistic support for individuals. Rooted in the tradition of continental European social theories, social pedagogy takes an integrative and inclusive perspective on education, emphasizing the importance of social interaction, personal growth, and societal involvement in the learning process. The main objective of social pedagogy is not merely the transmission of knowledge, but fostering the development of the whole person, supporting them to reach their full potential, and promoting their well-being in the broader social context.

A significant aspect of the social pedagogy perspective is the relationship between the pedagogue (educator) and the learner. The relationship is viewed as a mutual interaction, a dialogue, and a co-construction of knowledge, rather than a one-way transmission of information from the teacher to the student. This relationship-based practice is centered on humanistic values, and the pedagogue's role is to engage the learner in a democratic partnership, fostering a sense of belonging and active participation in the learning process.

Social pedagogy places a heavy emphasis on social justice, highlighting the importance of equality, inclusivity, and respect for diversity. The approach encourages learners to be socially engaged and active citizens, fostering a sense of responsibility and empathy towards others.

This perspective also recognizes the learning potential in everyday life situations, integrating formal, non-formal, and informal learning experiences. It encompasses a broad array of activities, such as play, arts, cultural activities, practical skills, and problem-solving tasks, which contribute to the learner's overall cognitive, emotional, social, and moral development.

Final thoughts

From a social pedagogue perspective, such as myself, assessment might take a more holistic form, considering not just academic performance but the overall growth of the learner. It would likely involve self-reflection, peer feedback, project-based assessments, and other forms of evaluation that capture the learner's progress in a variety of dimensions, from intellectual development to social and emotional competencies.

Critics might argue that social pedagogy's emphasis on holistic development and relationship-based practices can make it challenging to measure learning outcomes objectively. Furthermore, its integration into systems primarily focused on academic achievement may be difficult. Despite these challenges, the holistic, integrative, and inclusive approach of social pedagogy offers valuable insights for creating more equitable and comprehensive educational experiences.

Norm-Critical Pedagogy: A Revolutionary Shift in Swedish Education

Over the past decade, Sweden has witnessed a substantial shift in its educational landscape through the pervasive adoption of norm-critical pedagogy. This revolutionary teaching approach, rooted in feminist and post-structural theories, has strived to challenge and subvert ingrained power relations and both conscious and unconscious norms.

Tghrough my profession, I am at the heart of this transformation. I am committed to fostering a more tolerant and inclusive educational environment and classroom culture. My work is deeply embedded in norm-critical perspectives, pushing boundaries and challenging dominant norms to promote respect, understanding, and equal opportunities for all learners.

Moreover, as a mother of three boys, I also apply these principles at home. I educate them to be responsible, empathetic, and respectful individuals with an inclusive perspective. I strive to equip them with the critical thinking skills necessary to challenge the status quo and contribute positively to a diverse and inclusive society.

The term 'norm-critical pedagogy' was first introduced in the book "Normkritisk pedagogik — makt, lärande och strategier för förändring" (Bromseth & Darj, 2010) and its popularity has only grown since. From research studies to the publication of method books and the establishment of educational companies specializing in this field, the concept has diffused throughout the Swedish education system.

However, as is often the case with new concepts, the interpretation and understanding of norm-critical pedagogy have evolved and diversified. Its rapid dissemination has birthed multiple interpretations, sparking controversy and criticism, especially in media where the term 'norm-criticism' has often been associated with oppressive and authoritarian ideologies.

Despite the controversy, numerous preschools, schools, organizations, and businesses continue to employ norm-critical pedagogy. The Swedish National Agency for Education (Skolverket) has even emphasized its significance in combating discrimination. This dichotomy of perspectives on norm-critical pedagogy is indicative of two parallel yet opposing interpretations, with relatively little research conducted on the subject to date.

In Sweden, terms like 'norm-critical work,' 'norm-critical approach,' 'norm-creativity,' and 'norm-awareness' are often interchangeably used in discussions on the topic. As the concept continues to take root in fields beyond pedagogy, terms like 'norm-criticism' and even 'the norm critique' are increasingly applied.

The progression of norm-critical pedagogy in Sweden has paralleled certain societal changes over the past decade. In the process of transforming society's understanding and application of norm criticism, several societal processes have played pivotal roles.

Among these processes, juridification is particularly noteworthy. It signifies a societal trend in which certain phenomena become subject to legal regulation. This trend has been prevalent in the Swedish school system, contributing to the strengthening of the individual rights of students and increased attention to equal treatment.

Under this legal framework, issues that were traditionally handled through interpersonal interactions are now often escalated to legal authorities, altering how discrimination issues are handled in schools. This increased juridification risks reducing norm-critical pedagogy to a mere legalistic approach to protecting individuals from discrimination.

Another influential factor is the neoliberal influence on teachers' roles. The neoliberal currents have redefined human relationships and the relationships between individuals and society in economic terms, impacting how people interact and take responsibility for one another and society.

In conclusion, norm-critical pedagogy in Sweden has emerged as a potent tool to challenge and transform societal norms. However, the legislation with the increasing influence of neoliberal ideologies, it is essential to ensure that its fundamental aim of questioning power dynamics and unconscious norms does not get overshadowed.

Reflecting on Albert Bandura's Social Learning Theory

As a social pedagogue, it is my essential role to decode the mechanisms and intricate subtleties behind human behavior and skills. An understanding of how knowledge is acquired and internalized equips us better to shape human learning and foster positive behavior. This journey leads us to Albert Bandura, a psychologist whose revolutionary social learning theory has enriched our understanding of human learning in profound ways.

From our classrooms to our homes, we often observe that learning is a bidirectional process. It's not only us who learn from our environment; our actions, in turn, shape the environment around us. This symbiotic relationship, reflected in Bandura's quote, "Learning is bidirectional: we learn from our environment and our environment learns and changes thanks to our actions," underscores the importance of social interactions in the learning process.

The Scope of Social Learning

The process of learning is not simply a mechanical one, driven by imitation, conditioning, and rewards or punishment. It's an intricate tapestry of observation, imitation, and development within a social environment, guided by mental states that can facilitate or impede learning.

Albert Bandura's social learning theory, also known as observational or model learning, bridges the gap between traditional behaviorism and the cognitive approach to learning. It goes beyond the passive model of a learner as an empty box to be filled with external influences and restrictions. Instead, Bandura suggests that learners actively process information and evaluate the relationship between behavior and consequences.

Unraveling the Power of Observation: The Bobo Doll Experiment

Perhaps no study better illustrates the power of observational learning than Bandura's iconic Bobo Doll experiment. Conducted between 1961 and 1963, this experiment sought to demonstrate the impact of a role model on children's behavior. The results were crystal clear

— children exposed to aggressive role models were more likely to act aggressively.

Bandura identified three fundamental forms of observational learning:

1. A live model, such as a real person demonstrating a behavior.
2. Verbal instructions specify and describe behavior.
3. Symbolic methods, like fictional characters from books or films.

Influencing Factors in Social Learning

The interplay of cognitive and behavioral factors, Bandura's "bridge," is a key element in the social learning theory. It's not that we mimic everything we see. Thoughts precede imitation, and several influencing factors can promote imitative behavior or alternative response. These factors include:

The Environment

Our society, far from being homogeneous, comprises a diversity of environments and scenarios, some of which are conducive to learning, while others are inhibitory.

Attention

Before we can imitate a behavior, it needs to first catch our attention and interest, activating our mirror neurons.

Motivation

Motivation, the drive to perform certain behaviors we observe in others, plays a crucial role in the learning process.

Wrapping it Up

To sum it up, the theory of social learning is one of the most exciting advances in the realm of psychology. Thanks to Albert Bandura, one of the most respected experts in his field, we now better understand how we acquire knowledge and develop specific behaviors. We comprehend the interplay between external social processes and internal cognitive ones, and the ways in which we can unknowingly serve as role models to others.

A Deep Dive Into Pedagogy in a Postmodern Era

As a social pedagogue and writer, I often grapple with the task of bridging the gap between theoretical pedagogy and practical implementation. This article is my reflection on the interplay of these two domains, outlining how they shape our understanding of education and learning in our increasingly complex society.

The Swedish pedagogical tradition offers some insights, stemming from its multifaceted perspective of education, which includes an intrinsic relationship between theory and practice. Contrary to the view held by René Descartes, the architect of modern knowledge, theory, and practice aren't mutually exclusive or isolated domains. The theoretical framework of pedagogy isn't just an abstract construction of ideas, but a tool that guides practical pedagogical judgments.

Pedagogical theories

Pedagogical theories serve as conceptual maps, linguistic demarcations, and navigation aids for various educational activities and practitioners. They provide a comprehensive understanding of the human condition and its sociocultural contexts, indispensable for the execution of pedagogical strategies. In that respect, the question is: "How can we build a pedagogical theory grounded in practical realities?"

Understanding the intricate fabric of pedagogy requires examining politically governed educational institutions tasked with realizing pedagogical aspirations and goals. An analysis of the evolving knowledge landscape of pedagogy in a postmodern context presents an opportunity to explore the internal and external conditions that shape it.

Three birthmarks of pedagogy — humanistic education heritage, reflective social-oriented heritage, and empirical professional heritage — constitute the tension field that shapes the geographical and topographical contours of pedagogy. Each birthmark has evolved from dominant ideologies about knowledge production and application, steering the discourse towards pragmatic solutions and practical knowledge application. Pedagogical knowledge has evolved from an idea perspective to a critical examination of society and education and now, under increasing economic-political influence, to useful knowledge.

Pedagogical knowledge

Further, there is a transition from a continental to an Anglo-Saxon thought process in Swedish education and research policy. This transition has profound implications on the landscape of pedagogical knowledge, bringing about a reorganization in the approach towards knowledge generation. The continental approach focused on knowledge objects (theoretical concepts) whereas the Anglo-Saxon approach is more focused on study objects (the empirical study).

Under the pressure of providing useful knowledge for political decision-making and pedagogical practice, pedagogy is shifting from a discipline of education science and critical social science towards an empirical application science aligned with "science" principles. As a result, pedagogical topics are increasingly determined by study objects like high school education, elementary school teaching, and leadership in education, rather than shared knowledge objects and discourse.

The evolution of pedagogy as a scientific discipline took a significant turn in the late 19th century when it emerged in tandem with psychology. The first professor of pedagogy, Bertil Hammer, in his inaugural lecture on October 8, 1910, divided pedagogy into three parts: philosophical pedagogy, psychological pedagogy, and social pedagogy. These three areas have remained relevant throughout the 20th century and continue to guide the understanding of pedagogical practices in our times.

Final thoughts

In conclusion, pedagogy's strength lies in its ability to harmonize theory and practice. As social pedagogues, we have a responsibility to bridge this gap, fostering an environment where the theoretical informs the practical and vice versa. Embracing this approach, we can help shape an education system that is adaptable, dynamic, and responsive to the ever-evolving needs of our society.

Harnessing Behaviorism and Cognitivism for Better Teaching and Learning Outcomes

I'm not just a social pedagogue, I am someone who has delved deep into the intricate universe of learning theories and their practical applications, forever pursuing the noble goal of fostering understanding and growth.

My journey into social pedagogy is a testimony to the power of patience, dedication, and continuous learning. Like any seasoned traveler, I've used various theoretical maps to guide my journey. Specifically, I've spent considerable time studying four pivotal learning theories, namely, behaviorism, cognitivism, pragmatism, and the sociocultural perspective. Each one offers a unique lens to view and understand how teaching should be conducted and assessed.

Understanding Behaviorism

The roots of behaviorism lie in the empirical tradition, postulating that humans are born as blank slates, shaped by upbringing and experiences. In this paradigm, humans are seen as biological objects, with thoughts and feelings reduced to mere chemical reactions. A prominent figure in this field, Ivan Pavlov, popularized the concept of conditioning, most famously illustrated through his experiment with dogs — the "Pavlov's dogs" experiment.

Under the behaviorist perspective, humans learn different behaviors through associating stimuli with responses, a concept known as associationistic learning. This theory suggests that all human behaviors and development are founded on conditioning. B. F. Skinner expanded upon this idea, conceptualizing human behaviors in individual components, arguing that learning occurs step-by-step, shaped by rewards or punishments.

However, behaviorism isn't without its critics. Scholars like Noam Chomsky argued that behaviorism fails to explain the emergence or development of language and other creative processes. They contend that human learning extends beyond simple repetition and conditioning, thus leading to the evolution of a more rationalist perspective of knowledge — cognitivism.

Embracing Cognitivism

Cognitivism, predominantly associated with the researcher Jean Piaget, posits that humans are thinking beings capable of reasoning and developing new abilities independently. Piaget's theory suggests that humans construct knowledge and reality by observing and processing information from the environment, a process he termed 'assimilation'.

Furthermore, Piaget introduced the concept of 'accommodation', the ability to change our thinking and learning process when we encounter new information that conflicts with our existing knowledge. He proposed stages of cognitive development, which, despite its criticism for its rigidity and normative nature, remains influential in understanding the human learning process.

My Role as a Social Pedagogue

As a social pedagogue, I constantly dance between these theories, behaviorism, and cognitivism, understanding that each offers its unique insights and limitations. I believe in the flexibility of thought and approach, seeing these theories not as contradictions but as complementary pieces of a complex puzzle.

But it's not just about theory. I put this knowledge into practice, shaping my pedagogical approach to enhance learning outcomes. Like a seasoned traveler who has discovered the power of using different maps, I navigate the intricate landscape of human learning, drawing from these theories to create the best routes for my students.

In this dynamic and ever-evolving field of social pedagogy, my journey is characterized by continuous learning, adaptability, and a deep commitment to facilitating growth and understanding. I believe, as a social pedagogue, it's not just about what you teach; it's about how you teach it. It's about recognizing that every student is unique and that teaching, at its core, is about guiding each individual to unlock their potential.

Final Thoughts

Dear reader, I hope my journey as a social pedagogue inspires you to explore the intricate layers of human learning and appreciate the art and science behind teaching. Let us recognize the value of different learning theories, understand their nuances, and leverage their strengths in our pursuit of fostering meaningful learning experiences.

EMPOWERING STUDENTS Through Effective Feedback

As an integral part of assessment and learning processes, feedback can be verbal, written, or even conveyed through actions. However, the aim is to enhance a student's performance, not deter it. I've always felt that the process of providing feedback should be positive, or at the very least, a neutral learning experience for the student. Negative feedback can unfortunately discourage students and diminish their efforts and achievements. It falls upon us, educators, to carefully nurture a student's learning process and provide feedback in a manner that leaves them feeling inspired rather than defeated or frustrated.

Providing feedback means offering students an explanation of what they're doing well and where they can improve, with an emphasis on their strengths. It is most beneficial for students learning when they are guided on what is correct and what can be improved in their work. One technique I've found helpful is the 'praise, correct, praise' method.

Timing is crucial when it comes to feedback. I believe immediate feedback, given right after a student demonstrates a learning outcome, encourages a more positive response and reinforces their learning. Delayed feedback, on the other hand, might disconnect the learning moment from the feedback, causing a potential loss in its impact.

Moreover, tailoring feedback to the student's individual needs is essential. Classrooms are diverse, with students who have varying needs. Some need a gentle push to attain higher levels, while others need a more sensitive approach to ensure their self-esteem and enthusiasm for learning aren't compromised.

I recently read an enlightening article by Stephen Dinham titled "Feedback on feedback" in the Teacher Magazine, 2014. Studies show that students wish to know where they stand in their work. By consistently answering the following four questions, educators can offer valuable feedback:

1. What is the student doing well?
2. What is the student not doing so well?
3. How does the student's work compare to others?
4. How can the student improve?

One thing that I find particularly important is to communicate the purpose of the feedback to students. Show them what educators are looking for by providing them with examples of exemplary work and subpar work. This approach becomes increasingly important at higher learning levels.

Instead of merely justifying a grade, using comments to instruct is an effective method. The focus should be on what we'd like students to address in future work, and linking the feedback to the task's objectives.

Lastly, providing feedback to the entire class orally or in a shared written document, and not just individually, can also be beneficial.

Rethinking the Classroom and Making Learning Accessible

Every day, I work with children and observe their learning journeys. My insights are grounded in my professional and personal experiences, as well as in established research.

But first, let's clarify — what does 'accessibility' mean? According to Myndigheten för delaktighet (the Swedish Agency for Participation), accessibility is about how society is designed. An accessible organization is one designed in such a way that as many people as possible can use and participate in it. This is precisely how a classroom should also be structured. Don't you agree?

With the insights I've gleaned from my work and life, as well as the lessons from a course assignment, I've developed some ideas for improving classroom accessibility.

The Timing Factor: Reframing the Lunch-to-Lesson Transition

One reflection revolves around the timing of lessons. Some schools schedule mathematics lessons right after lunch. From observing my children, particularly my youngest son who is just six years old, I've noted that this timing could burden metacognitive abilities. We risk burdening metacognitive abilities by placing a math lesson immediately after lunch. Metacognition refers to being aware of one's own thinking and acting based on it. It involves interpreting, evaluating, reflecting, and problem-solving by the situation, purpose, or context.

When our bodies are trying to digest food, they direct more blood toward the stomach, resulting in less blood — and consequently, less oxygen — for the brain. This can burden our analytical abilities. In an article titled "Därför tappar vi farten efter lunch" (Why we slow down after lunch) by Kerstin Petersson, Arne Lowden, associate professor at the Stress Research Institute, Stockholm University, explains why efficiency decreases after lunch. The article points out how postprandial (after meal) fatigue often occurs because energy is mobilized for digestion at the expense of, for example, brainwork.

Noise, Stress, and Learning: A Correlation?

Another factor worth considering is the level of noise during lunch breaks. An article titled "Ny forskning: Stressiga måltider påverkar inlärning" (New research: Stressful meals affect learning) by Maria

Ehrlin highlights research from Umeå suggesting high noise levels in the dining hall can cause stress and poor eating habits among students. This, in turn, can lead to poorer performance in school.

The Mathematics Challenge: Accessibility in Numbers

Moreover, the subject of mathematics has shown a negative trend in results for several years (Skolverket 2016c). About 89% of 6th-grade students have met the requirements for the math test, and about 84% of 9th-grade students have met the math test requirements. This evidence points to the need for better accessibility and effectiveness in our approach to teaching mathematics.

Creating Accessibility in Mathematics: A Pedagogical Challenge

An article titled "Att skapa tillgänglighet till matematik — vilka är de pedagogiska utmaningarna?" (Creating Accessibility in Mathematics — What are the Pedagogical Challenges?) by Helena Roos and Ann-Louise Ljungblad, suggests that one of the reasons students have difficulties with learning in mathematics could be medical/neurological causes, such as ADHD, Autism, Aspergers, and Tourette's syndrome, which affect learning.

Additionally, students with reading and writing difficulties can need help with mathematical text. The researchers argue that there is a connection between language ability and cognitive ability. The authors further assert that mathematics requires effort and hard work, and it's essential that our education system facilitates learning and takes into account how scheduling impacts mathematics lesson study results.

Illuminating the Corners of Welfare Models

It's always a joy to share my professional journey with you and I want to delve deeper into the realm of welfare models — their origins, unique characteristics, and their respective challenges and opportunities.

Through this article, we'll embark on a fascinating journey that starts from the foundation of welfare states and travels through three distinct models of welfare, touching upon their impacts on retired and unemployed groups.

At the heart of a welfare state, as outlined in Mikael Bruér's article "The Swedish Welfare", is the assurance of citizens' economic and social well-being, generally financed by mandatory fees intended to support individuals during periods of heightened need. It is a concept common to most advanced industrialized countries, but the specifics vary, creating different world models for different groups in need. In the Swedish context, welfare is primarily financed through taxes that cater to various societal needs such as education, elder care, and healthcare — embodying the fundamental principle of welfare regimes.

Exploring the arena of welfare theories and models, the SO-rummet podcast, "Välfärdsteorier och välfärdsmodeller" by Julia Matsson, Kristofer Larsson and Mattias Axelson, discusses the three welfare models: the liberal, the social democratic, and the conservative.

The Liberal Welfare Model, heavily present in countries like the USA, Australia, and the UK, strongly emphasizes the free market and individualism. Historically formed during the "great transformation" in the wake of the industrial revolution, it has its roots in England. A primary challenge here for the unemployed is to meet the condition of being "actively seeking work" to qualify for unemployment benefits. A benefit of this model is that due to low taxation, individuals can self-finance their own unemployment compensation, retirement, or healthcare. Pensioners, in this system, may face the burden of self-financing their retirement to a greater extent.

The Social Democratic Welfare Model, dominant in Nordic countries like Sweden, Norway, Denmark, Finland, and Iceland, focuses on social equality and redistribution. The protection of workers and the promotion of full employment are at its heart. However, the requirement to have worked for a continuous period before being eligible for unemployment benefits can be challenging for some individuals. Pensioners are more secure under this model as they benefit from a tax-financed public pension, with the option for an individual pension supplemented by an employer-paid occupational pension.

Lastly, the Conservative Welfare Model, which is a transformation of pre-industrial forms, has its unique set of challenges and opportunities. The Conservative Welfare Model is characterized by 1) organized group politics, 2) a societal economy, and 3) mutual social policy. This model is essentially a remnant of pre-industrial feudal forms, particularly those later transformed and codified based on the social foundation of the Roman Catholic Church.

The model finds its roots in the preservation of traditional societal structures and hierarchies. It maintains the stratification in society, and the level of welfare benefits is often linked to the social status of the individual and their history of contributions. In this model, social insurance is funded by contributions from employers and employees rather than general taxation.

This model is prevalent in continental European countries, which include nations like Germany, France, Italy, Belgium, and the Netherlands. Unemployment benefits and pensions under the Conservative Welfare Model are related to earning levels and length of employment, which means the unemployed and the elderly might face unique challenges if they have not had stable, long-term employment.

Each welfare model, in its unique way, addresses the varying needs of different groups, including the pensioners and the unemployed. For example, as illustrated in the podcast, "Swedish Welfare Structures and How They Work", pensioners in Sweden have a secure safety net in the form of a public pension that is fully tax-financed. Simultaneously, they also have the option to contribute to their pension, supplemented by the employer-paid occupational pension.

In conclusion, while each model has its unique strengths and challenges, a common thread runs through them all — the welfare state's commitment to ensuring the economic and social well-being of its citizens, particularly those most in need, such as the unemployed and pensioners. As a social pedagogue, understanding these models helps me in my advocacy work, providing support and championing the rights of those I work with.

Safeguarding Children's Rights in Sweden

I wish to share with you my experiences, my concerns, and the critical roles each of us plays in safeguarding children's rights in our society.

In 2020, a significant milestone was reached in Sweden: the UN Convention on the Rights of the Child became Swedish law, affirming that all children are of equal value and entitled to their rights. This law is a testament to our commitment to protect and empower our youngest citizens, and it's something I take immense pride in. But, what does this really mean for our children? Are they well-protected in Sweden?

Are Children Well-Protected in Sweden?

In my perspective, a resounding yes echoes throughout our society. We've paid tremendous attention to embedding the Child Convention's principles in our school laws, curriculums, activities, and values. Our preschools and schools shoulder a great responsibility in recognizing and acting upon any suspicion of child abuse, always ready to report and intervene when necessary. For a deeper look into the Convention, visit UNICEF's page about it.

Yet, despite the strong framework we've built, there is no room for complacency. We can and should always strive to make things better.

Who is Responsible for Upholding a Child's Rights?

The responsibility of ensuring children's rights does not rest with the state, regions, and municipalities alone. It extends to private entities that provide state services concerning children — including independent schools and healthcare institutions. Of course, parents or other guardians play a vital role in the child's upbringing and development, guiding them in realizing their rights.

What Could be Improved in our Laws?

Having studied the Social Services Act and the Child Convention extensively, I appreciate the thorough and protective measures they provide for children. However, one aspect that might benefit from further strengthening relates to the adults responsible for children. In many cases, it's the very people they trust most that let them down. Their caretakers — be they parents, foster families, educators, representatives, coaches, or leaders — become the perpetrators.

It's a sobering reality that underscores the critical need for everyone involved in a child's life to remain vigilant and committed to their welfare. And this is where I, as a social pedagogue, along with my peers, step in. Our mission is to foster a safe, supportive, and nurturing environment for our children, upholding their rights and protecting them from harm.

Reasoning on the matter

The journey toward child protection is an ongoing process, one that requires the involvement and commitment of all stakeholders. As a social pedagogue, I'll continue to advocate for our children's rights, strive for their well-being, and work towards a society where every child is safe, cared for, and empowered to reach their potential. Together, let's create a world where children truly are our most treasured asset.

Empathy, Understanding, and Social Skills to Address Global Challenges

My journey as a social pedagogue began with witnessing the scarcity of necessities such as housing, healthcare, clean water, and education in many regions globally. The inequitable distribution of resources was not a mere statistic for me; it became a lived experience as I encountered countless individuals grappling with this harsh reality every day. This wasn't just a professional encounter — it was a deeply personal realization of the world's uneven development and the pressing need for change.

Hunger, a global crisis, became an urgent call to action in my journey. Every life lost to malnutrition, every person part of the 10% of our global population affected, was a stark reminder of the education and information vacuum that fuels this vicious cycle of poverty and hunger.

One particular encounter that left an indelible mark on my heart was witnessing child abuse. The heart-wrenching instances of exploitation, often rooted in poverty, threw light on the complexity of social issues we face and the need for systemic solutions rather than isolated ones.

In my interactions with the victims of sexual and racial discrimination, I realized that the pain and suffering caused by these societal plagues run deep and affect countless lives. Despite the persistent challenges, these experiences also revealed the transformative power of social pedagogy to foster understanding, empathy, and collaboration.

Through these experiences, I've come to appreciate social skills as more than theoretical concepts — they are lifelines. These essential behavioral strategies have the potential to reshape individual lives and entire societies. They empower us to respectfully express our emotions, desires, and opinions, improving our interpersonal relationships and allowing us to achieve our goals without infringing on others.

In my career and personal life, I have seen the impact of social skills in every environment — in families, workplaces, and schools. They've allowed me to understand others and express myself, consider everyone's needs, and offer support when needed.

This journey has been both arduous and rewarding. I have dedicated myself to empowering others with the social skills needed to navigate our complex global society's issues. Despite the monumental challenges, I remain optimistic because I've seen change happen — one interaction, one conversation, one story at a time.

It is this optimism and resolve that fuel my journey in social pedagogy — a journey towards a more equitable world that starts with each one of us. Harnessing our collective social abilities, I firmly believe that we can make strides in addressing these global challenges.

The Learning Environment for Students with Cognitive Challenges

I can attest to the importance of creating the right environment for our children to learn effectively. This experience has been shaped not just by my journey but also by thorough research and pedagogical studies. One critical area I've found significant is the pace of learning in our classrooms.

Living in an era of high speed and multi-tasking can be particularly challenging for students struggling with cognitive functions such as executive, metacognitive abilities, and analytical skills. A high-paced classroom environment can intensify these challenges. As educators and parents, we need to understand the impacts of these factors on our children's learning processes.

Slowing down the pace in classrooms allows students to better develop trust in their abilities and mastery over foundational concepts, such as mathematical thinking. This perspective is affirmed by the Swedish Curriculum for the Compulsory School, Preschool Class, and the Leisure-time Center 2022 (Lgr 22), which highlights the need for students to be able to formulate, solve problems, and evaluate chosen strategies.

In their 2020 article from the Swedish National Agency for Education, authors Judit Simon and Ulf Jederlund of Stockholm University explain that "The small steps simplify the process, as it's enough to focus on a single small step at a time rather than stressing over the whole". This sentiment resonates with my experiences as well.

Autism educator and lecturer Lotta Abrahamsson echoes this sentiment in her lecture "UR Samtiden — ADHD — help how do you do?". She notes that children exposed to high-paced environments with a constant influx of information and various stimuli can experience a negative impact on their self-confidence, development, learning, and social adjustments.

Furthermore, providing simple, step-by-step instructions or creating a checklist can significantly aid students' comprehension. This is because executive function, associated with the frontal lobes of the brain, serves as our cognitive control system. In her article "To support executive functions", psychologist Gunilla Carlsson Kendall describes how cognitive abilities are strained in children with functional impairments and suggests the practice of breaking down tasks into smaller parts.

Similarly, the Swedish National Agency for Education emphasizes the need for teachers to concretize the knowledge requirements in relation to the chosen knowledge content to make learning outcomes more explicit. This is further supported by David Edfelt, a licensed psychologist and author of "Autism and ADHD in high school — clarifying pedagogy," who advises breaking up a large task into several smaller ones to make the task more manageable.

By creating an environment that slows down the pace and provides clear instructions, we can better cater to our children's cognitive capabilities, thereby enhancing their learning experiences.

The Art of Leading and Empowering Neurodiverse Children and Young Adults

Life is a continuous journey of learning and evolving. For me, this journey has led me into the heart of social pedagogy, where I've found my purpose — to be a guiding light, an advocate, and a bridge-builder for children and young adults with neurodevelopmental disorders (NDD).

As a social pedagogue, my work revolves around providing support to students, parents, and teachers concerning various social issues. Our role is diverse, ranging from fostering inclusive environments, working preventatively, promoting overall well-being, and supporting academic and social education. My recent lecture on NDD was a testament to this, emphasizing the art of guiding neurodiverse children and young adults.

Safety and security form the bedrock of any learning environment. As part of my responsibilities, I work closely with school staff to cultivate a nurturing environment. We organize social activities, supervise during break times, conduct safety walks, and employ group-strengthening activities. The goal? To create a safer, welcoming space for both students and staff.

The qualities that are pivotal in succeeding as a social pedagogue are responsibility, confidence, and an unwavering passion for creating secure educational spaces. It requires a level of personal maturity and courage to navigate difficult conversations with students and their guardians. Even under immense pressure, it's crucial to remain professional and patient.

Lately, at least in Sweden, social pedagogy has evolved within the framework of our welfare system and social care. It's centered around listening to student needs, promoting inclusion, addressing students' health and mental well-being, preventing exclusion and marginalization, and supporting academic and social education. As a social pedagogue, my ultimate goal is to see the entire student, support their social needs, boost motivation, and work preventatively with those at risk. I hope that every school will soon employ trained personnel, preferably social pedagogues, who can ensure that all children's rights are upheld.

Something that struck me recently is the tone of verbal feedback and its crucial role in how it is received. An aggressive or sharp tone can lead children to shut down and lose focus. Hence, it's important to maintain a calm and serious demeanor, particularly when delivering feedback that might not be easy to hear. As sensitive beings, children may only need to hear the less positive aspects once to initiate a change in behavior.

In the role of a social pedagogue, I believe that remaining calm regardless of the type of feedback you're delivering — positive or constructive — is crucial. This approach, paired with guiding students considerately, can prove quite effective.

Constructive criticism is indeed important, but there's a significant difference between saying, "You are dumb" and "That was not a wise choice." As social pedagogues, we hold a position of power and must use feedback to encourage positive traits in students. This responsibility becomes more critical when dealing with teenagers, as poorly chosen words can have detrimental effects. A good approach might be to start with praise, highlight areas of improvement, and end with further praise.

As I continue to learn and grow in my role, my goal is to master the art of delivering constructive criticism effectively. Through practice and the ongoing education I'm receiving, I am confident I will find the perfect recipe for delivering beneficial feedback to my students. Together, we can build a more inclusive, supportive, and nurturing learning environment for all.

The Many Facets of Knowledge

The world of knowledge unfolds before me like an endless horizon. It's not just about facts or figures, but a rich tapestry woven with threads of understanding, awareness, and insight. This journey through knowledge is a conscious and deliberate act of understanding, of knowing.

There are myriad types of knowledge that we, as human beings, come to acquire throughout our lives. The quest to decipher the truth and gather evidence is integral to this journey. To understand how we gain knowledge, we first need to understand what truth is.

Empirical knowledge

This type of knowledge is acquired through our senses and provides us with experiential insights. It's the aroma of a freshly brewed cup of coffee, a roaring fire crackle, or a rose petal's silky touch.

Scientific knowledge

Whose purpose is to explain reality and natural phenomena. It seeks to unveil the mysteries of the universe, from the atomic to the cosmic level.

Mathematical knowledge

An abstract creation of our minds. It isn't derived from sensory perception but forms the backbone of logical reasoning and problem-solving.

Emotional knowledge

Knowledge isn't just confined to these quantifiable realms. Emotional knowledge is vital for our personal growth and relationships with others. It helps us navigate the complex world of human emotions and allows us to empathize and connect with others on a deeper level.

So, how does one know they've acquired knowledge?

Through testing, encouragement, prompting, and questioning. Interaction is key. We learn not just by absorbing information, but by engaging with it, questioning it, and applying it.

How does one ascertain if another person has acquired knowledge?

Again, through questioning, testing, and prompting. It's through interaction and action that we can evaluate others' understanding and knowledge.

Can one lose the knowledge they once acquired?

Indeed, forgetting is a part of the learning process. I, for instance, have forgotten many mathematical concepts I once learned. If we don't use certain knowledge regularly, there's a risk of forgetting it.

Is all knowledge good knowledge?

In my opinion, all knowledge is good knowledge, but not all knowledge is beneficial for everyone. Each person is unique. We often learn information that we never end up using in our lives. In that sense, one could say that knowledge has an expiration date. It reminds me of Jean Piaget's words: "Intelligence is what you use when you don't know what to do."

Does knowledge have a "best before" date?

I wouldn't necessarily call it a "best before" date. It's more about seizing the opportunities to apply knowledge at the right place, right time, and right context.

Can knowledge be harmful to individuals or groups?

How and for what purpose we use knowledge can make it harmful. Knowledge itself is neutral; it's our application of it that can be beneficial or detrimental.

As for my personal learning process, I thrive on a highly organized structure and fixed routines. Whether it's studying or working, these habits help me immensely. In my learning process, I always follow a study plan with specific objectives. I wake up quite early in the morning and ensure that I study for at least a few uninterrupted hours every day. This includes reading course literature, taking notes, and searching for necessary information on the internet.

Learning is a journey, and as a social pedagogue, my mission is to make this journey as enlightening and enriching as possible for the learners I guide. Walk with me on this path of knowledge and discovery.

The Power of Support and Adaptation in The Classroom

The transformative power of additional support in our classrooms it is a support that often takes the form of a resource person such as a student assistant, a social pedagogue, or a teacher assistant. These professionals play a vital role in our education system, helping students who need extra support due to functional impairments. They catch these students' attention and assist them in focusing on the tasks at hand.

According to paragraph 11 of the Swedish Education Act, under special circumstances, decisions can be made for a student in basic school, a particular school, or Sami school to receive special support individually or in a different teaching group than the one the student usually belongs to (Skollagen, 2010, 13). Yet, support doesn't end there.

Adapting the Learning Pathway

Under Paragraph 12 of the Swedish Education Act, if the special support for a student cannot be reasonably adapted to their needs and conditions, a decision can lead to deviations from the timetable, subjects, and goals that otherwise apply to the education — what's termed an 'adapted study path' (Skollagen, 2010, 13). The headmaster is responsible for ensuring that a student with an adapted study path receives an education that is equivalent to the regular education in the school form (Skollagen, 2010, 13).

Creating a Visually Accessible Classroom: The TEACCH Approach

Beyond additional support and adaptive pathways, visual accessibility also plays a key role in educational accessibility. Ensuring equal treatment to avoid visual difficulties and decreased transmission of correct information and instructions to students is paramount. Without it, the student's ability to handle information can be strained due to the risk of receiving incorrect or incomplete instructions.

For instance, the TEACCH method (Treatment and Education of Autistic and Communication Handicapped Children), mentioned in the course material book "Autism and ADHD in high school:

clarifying pedagogy", can significantly improve visual learning. This teaching method, developed at the University of North Carolina by Dr. Eric Schopler and Dr. Robert Reichler in the 1960s, provides a structured form of visual learning, also known as clarifying pedagogy in Sweden.

The TEACCH method is tailored to each autistic child's difficulties, taking into account all characteristic traits of autism. This nuanced approach acknowledges that every autistic child is unique and requires personalized teaching strategies.

A key component of the TEACCH method is its use of visual aids, which can significantly enhance a child's understanding of tasks and routines. This visual structuring assists students in organizing their day and allows for easier transitions between tasks, fostering independence and confidence.

Furthermore, these visual cues can be particularly beneficial for non-verbal children who may struggle with traditional teaching methods. By presenting information in a clear, visual format, the TEACCH method helps these children to better grasp complex concepts and feel more engaged in their learning.

The Impact of Inclusive Strategies

Reflecting on my experience as a social pedagogue and as a mother of three boys, one of whom is just six years old, I can assert that the inclusive strategies we employ in our education system have a profound impact. The additional support, adaptive study paths, and visual accessibility measures not only provide necessary assistance to students with special needs but also enrich the learning environment for all students.

Children learn from each other. A classroom that celebrates diversity and uses a variety of teaching methods benefits everyone. It fosters empathy, understanding, and mutual respect among students while equipping them with the skills to navigate a diverse world.

Looking Forward

As we move forward, it's crucial to continue enhancing these strategies. Just as we adapt our teaching methods to better serve our students, we too must evolve with the changing times. The measures we take today will directly impact our children's tomorrow.

From Plato to Present: The Evolving Role of Social Pedagogy in Our Society

The subject of pedagogy and its societal interpretation holds a particular resonance for me. We will trace the roots of social pedagogy from the philosophies of Plato and Aristotle to its modern-day applications, offering a rich perspective on how it shapes our society.

Historically, pedagogy has been intertwined with society, a notion going back to the teachings of Plato and Aristotle. Both philosophers saw no difference between society and state or between social pedagogy and political pedagogy.

Plato's social theory was founded on economic and ethical principles, dividing society into three classes: workers, warriors, and wise philosophers who would govern the state, as described in his dialogues in "The Republic".

Aristotle's approach to social pedagogy was intermixed with political pedagogy. His views were more grounded in the reality of the historical society he lived in. A realist and conservative, Aristotle conceived education in two phases: upbringing from birth, primarily within the family, followed by state-led education.

Fast forward to the present day, pedagogy has evolved into a social science focused on learning motivation, knowledge acquisition, and fostering constructive thinking. It is a continuous development in society's educational systems and teaching methodologies, combining knowledge from various fields like sociology, history, philosophy, and psychology. Modern pedagogy encompasses upbringing, interaction, and community-building.

In the realm of social pedagogy, we delve into the theoretical science and discipline within social education, targeting both individuals and groups grappling with adaptation problems, marginalization, or social difficulties. Social pedagogy employs strategies to aid and support the social integration of individuals while respecting human rights. It studies social work and offers a targeted pedagogy for children and youths.

The goal of social pedagogy is to enhance individuals' social skills and their learning of all essential social competencies to become functioning individuals in today's society. Social pedagogues are needed in a variety of areas, such as preschool education, family support, youth work, non-academic adult education, disability care, and workplace environments.

The field of social pedagogy even extends into other professional areas, including family support, sociocultural-environmental education, and cultural heritage management.

In essence, social pedagogy's purpose is to prepare individuals for life within society. It focuses on the development of moral and ethical values, enabling individuals to integrate into their culture and community and to live in unity. It requires collaboration between the pedagogue and the individual, emphasizing community as a necessary and extremely important part of life.

As we venture into the future, let's remember that social pedagogy, in its myriad forms, is a crucial component of our societal fabric, threading together the principles of learning, compassion, and community.

Understanding and Implementing Effective Learning Strategies

A social pedagogue's journey is steeped in the complexities and wonders of learning — the process of acquiring knowledge, skills, values, and attitudes through studies, teaching, or experiences. My passion lies not just in teaching, but in fostering environments where learning comes alive. Every child's mind is a library waiting to be filled, and as a social pedagogue, I am in a unique position to help curate its contents.

Learning, as described by behavioral psychology, is evidenced by changes observed in a subject's behavior. A fundamental process of learning is imitation, the repetition of a monitored process involving time, space, skills, and other resources. Through imitation, children learn the basic tasks required to function in society.

But what does this look like in practice?

Learning is often defined as the relatively permanent change in a person's behavior as a result of experience. My role is to facilitate these experiences, to guide children as they explore and understand the world around them.

The planning phase is key to developing desired student skills or performing well in class for a teacher. It encompasses the objectives (the skills), the content, methodical alternatives, educational strategies, the literature/textbooks, and the materials. Everything that is needed for "successful" learning.

The teaching process requires meticulous planning and a careful selection of additional resources relative to the curriculum's content. To achieve effective learning, I as an educator must consider aspects such as content, process, evaluation, and learning environment.

Identifying a student's strengths and weaknesses, understanding the curriculum's structure and adjusting it for successful learning, and utilizing digital tools, and various pedagogical applications — all these are fundamental in my approach to learning. Efficient planning of teaching resources and learning techniques is pivotal. And before one starts studying, it's essential to motivate oneself to simplify the journey.

The place of study is important too. Avoid distractions and manage your time effectively. A conducive school environment is crucial for students learning with the infrastructure, development of pedagogical and didactic programs, and proper use of technology.

Life in itself is the best teacher. If we didn't learn from our experiences, it wouldn't be our learning, but that of the people who lived the experience. Only through experiences, and accepting mistakes and failures, can we draw our conclusions to progress.

Is there such a thing as people who are better at learning and people who are worse at learning?

In my experience, there are no "good" or "bad" learners, only different learning methods. Some students are visual learners, responding to images and drawings. Others are auditory learners, who learn best through listening. Some prefer reading and writing, while others are kinesthetic learners, learning best through action and interaction. I firmly believe it's about finding the right method for each student or child.

In the garden of knowledge, every child blooms at their own pace and in their unique way. As a social pedagogue, my job is to provide the right environment, the right tools, and the right support to make each blooming a spectacular event. Together, let's embrace the beauty and complexity of learning.

Challenging Stereotypes and Nurturing Resilience in Schools

In a world as diverse interconnected as ours, one might wonder why stereotypes and biases still persist, particularly in the realm of education. As an ardent advocate for equality and inclusivity, I find myself consistently grappling with this issue. The pages of my personal story are filled with observations, experiences, and a growing understanding of the challenges our education system faces and the solutions we can harness to overcome them.

The Swedish National Agency for Education's book "Promote, Prevent, Detect, and Act" provides a comprehensive guide for schools to counter discrimination and bullying. It outlines four steps: monitoring, analysis and assessment, planning, and implementation. It underscores the importance of developing clear guidelines and routines to combat harassment, absenteeism, drug use, and other challenges in schools.

But beyond these guidelines lies a deeper challenge — the prevalence of deeply ingrained negative stereotypes about minority groups among teachers, parents, students, and other stakeholders. These stereotypes, considered "normal" to an alarming extent, can influence the behavior and attitudes of students and educators alike.

Think about it this way: How many times have we dismissed harmful "jokes" or actions as "boys being boys" or shrugged off stereotypical portrayals of genders in textbooks? These seemingly minor instances reinforce bias and aggressive behavior among students, lower expectations from teachers, and can even spawn negative attitudes from parents.

Eliminating stereotypes in schools is a daunting task, not least because their origins lie in society at large. This problem is magnified by the hate rhetoric, fake news, and conspiracy theories that pervade our digital media. Add to this the fact that minority groups are often underrepresented in school staff, and we are left with an education system that lacks the intercultural competence to create inclusive and quality learning environments.

How then, can we combat these issues? A part of the solution lies in promoting dialogue between schools and parents, even when linguistic barriers exist. This could mean making extra efforts to involve parents in school activities or ensuring that we have bilingual or multilingual staff to bridge the communication gap.

Moreover, we need to make inclusivity the heart of our education system. This means using inclusive language, embedding human rights and democratic citizenship in our curriculum, and encouraging discussions on controversial issues to give voice to our students. It means welcoming parents, building partnerships with community organizations, and, most importantly, learning from our students.

As a Social Pedagogue, I aim to keep integrating these principles into my work. My journey towards fostering a more inclusive and understanding education environment is ongoing. However, I am driven by the knowledge that each step taken is a step closer to nurturing resilient students who are prepared to thrive in our diverse world.

We have a long road ahead, but I am optimistic. By challenging stereotypes, promoting inclusivity, and appreciating diversity, we can shape the future of education for the better. And that is a future worth fighting for.

The Role of the Big Five in Future Pedagogy and Leadership

I've always been fascinated by the different aspects of human personality and how they play out in our daily interactions. This curiosity led me to delve into the Big Five personality theory, a scientific model that outlines five core traits defining our personality: Neuroticism, Extraversion, Openness, Conscientiousness, and Agreeableness. Today, I'd love to share how this journey deepened my understanding of Conscientiousness, Openness, and Extraversion, and has significantly impacted my practice in social pedagogy.

Conscientiousness: The Backbone of Pedagogy and Leadership

In my experience as a social pedagogue, conscientiousness has proven to be a crucial trait. This dimension of the personality involves elements such as being thorough, vigilant, and having a strong desire to perform tasks well. Self-discipline, a key facet of conscientiousness, is especially crucial when facing stressful situations where reliability matters most.

A conscientious leader ensures tasks are delegated appropriately and completed diligently. They consider the impacts of their decisions and address social issues within their domain with thoughtfulness and dedication.

Openness: A Tool for Adaptability in Pedagogy

The trait of openness to experience was another facet that deeply resonated with me. It represents active imagination, aesthetic sensitivity, attentiveness to inner feelings, a preference for variety, and intellectual curiosity. In our constantly evolving educational landscape, this trait is paramount for adaptability.

A teacher's willingness to experience and adapt, underpinned by this trait, showcases their creativity, curiosity, and resourcefulness, especially when dealing with unexpected occurrences within the learning environment.

Extraversion: Igniting Confidence in Leadership

The importance of extraversion, another trait, is particularly emphasized in my role as a pedagogue and leader. This personality dimension encapsulates the ability to confidently express oneself, be decisive, and inspire action — all of which significantly influence every member of a group or class.

Indeed, "confidence is contagious," but so is self-doubt. A teacher who harbors self-doubt may inadvertently spread this insecurity to their students. However, decisive action fueled by confidence can inspire students, especially those grappling with self-assurance, reassuring them that they are on the right track. Extraversion helps leaders exert influence, even through basic social interactions.

Incorporating Personality Traits into My Practice

The understanding of these personality factors — conscientiousness, openness to experience, and extraversion — has not only enriched my personal perspective but also empowered my role as a social pedagogue. As I continue in my profession, I see these traits as integral tools that I will continue to harness and refine to enhance my practice and the learning experiences of my students.

Through this personal exploration into the realm of the Big Five theory, I hope to inspire you, dear readers, to delve deeper into understanding your personality traits and how they may shape your interactions, decisions, and leadership style. After all, the journey toward personal growth and effective leadership begins with self-understanding.

As we forge ahead in our respective paths, let's embrace the wisdom encapsulated in the famous words of Socrates: "Know thyself." For me, it's not just a philosophical statement but a guidepost that illuminates my journey as a social pedagogue, igniting exciting possibilities. I hope it does the same for you!

Understanding and Validating Feelings for Effective Parenting

I am personally and professionally connected to the world of emotions, relationships, and personal growth. Your journey in understanding your children's emotions, fostering positive interactions, and empowering yourself is close to my heart. I want to share some essential insights on positive emotions, validation, and how they can profoundly impact our lives and those of our children.

Embracing Positive Emotions

Our emotions are not merely reactions to external stimuli; they are guiding forces that ensure our necessary needs for protection, safety, and care. More than fear and anxiety, positive emotions like joy, love, and curiosity guide us to act functionally in our relationships with others.

These emotions are expressed in our body language, facial expressions, and actions. By understanding and expressing what we feel, we can affirm and support others, especially our children.

Validation: Seeing and Accepting

Validation is an act of showing awareness and acceptance of another person. As a parent, you can confirm your child's emotions without letting them dictate your actions. Statements like "I see that you're struggling now... we just have to keep going a bit further" are examples of validating yet guiding responses.

Self-validation, particularly when support from the surroundings is lacking, involves having a non-judgmental attitude toward oneself. It means taking yourself seriously and encouraging, affirming, and supporting yourself in difficult situations.

Connecting Emotions and Thoughts

Emotions and thoughts are intertwined, and the basal parts of the brain, like the cerebellum and occipital lobe, activate when we react emotionally. Sometimes, sensory information can go directly to the "emotion center," allowing us to react emotionally before we even understand why.

While this mechanism can be advantageous in real threats, it can also create problems, making it challenging to think clearly during intense emotional reactions.

Children's Behavior and Learning

Wadström (2004) explains that behavior arises from the individual, and humans have an adaptability, unlike any other creatures. Webster—Stratton (2004) suggests that it is normal for children to have behavior problems. By addressing them correctly and patiently, many issues can be resolved.

Evenshaug & Hallen (2001) emphasize the importance of self-image in children's learning development. A child's self-conception, self-esteem and the view they have of themselves affect their learning achievements.

Behavior Analysis: A Three-Step Approach

Wadström (2004) proposes a three-step approach to behavior analysis. It involves determining the behavior or reaction, finding what triggers it, and understanding its reinforcements. This method helps in shaping and guiding children's behavior in a constructive way.

Final thoughts

Emotions are not enemies; they are essential for our survival. The more we expose ourselves to emotional reactions, the better we become at regulating and handling them.

In embracing our children's emotions and validating them, we are not just building bridges of trust and understanding; we are also teaching them essential life skills.

As you continue this beautiful journey of parenting, may you find strength, wisdom, and joy in each step.

The Power of Rhetoric and Its Role in Modern Education

As a both parent and pedagogue, I find myself intrigued by the power and importance of rhetoric in our daily lives and educational systems. Drawing from my personal experiences and the rich history of rhetoric, this article aims to explore the complex relationship between rhetoric, democracy, and education, with a focus on its resurgence in Swedish schools.

The Essence of Rhetoric

By rhetoric, we mean the knowledge of speaking convincingly, not the actual use. It's an art form that originated as a means of power alongside democracy in ancient Greece and still serves as a systematic study of influential communication. Nowadays, we still talk about rhetoric as the ability to speak correctly and choose the right tools, especially in speeches, but also in other communication situations.

Rhetoric's Birth and Development

Rhetoric can be traced back to the 5th century BCE in Athens, where a new form of ruler emerged — one that gained power not through physical superiority but through eloquence. In ancient Greece's direct democracy, the free men gathered to discuss critical matters, and the most persuasive speakers won support for their proposals. As Sigrell (2013, s. 14) puts it, "Language became a power factor, as sharp and double-edged as any sword."

Aristotle, one of rhetoric's great men, defined rhetoric as "the art of finding what, in every situation, is meant to convince." This definition encapsulates the knowledge and study of speaking correctly and persuasively.

Rhetoric and Democracy: A Historic Connection

Throughout history, rhetoric has been a vital tool for participation in societal debate. During antiquity, there was a strong link between rhetoric and democracy, as good speaking skills were essential for voicing opinions and influencing decisions. This connection persists in modern society and schools, where the art of expressing opinions through speech becomes increasingly essential.

Rhetoric in Swedish Schools

In Sweden, rhetoric once held a strong position in the education system. However, during the 1800s, it was removed as a separate subject. With the growing need for persuasive communication in various professions, there has been a resurgence of interest in rhetoric, leading to its reintegration into modern Swedish schools. Current curriculums emphasize the importance of rhetoric, fostering critical thinking and enabling students to make their voices heard in various contexts.

The comparison between Lpf94 and Lgy11, two educational plans in Sweden, reveals that rhetoric has gained a more prominent role in recent times. The Lgy11 plan specifically mentions rhetoric in several courses, reinforcing the importance of rhetorical skills in modern education.

Final Thoughts

The history of rhetoric is rich and compelling, and its application in modern education is undeniable. From ancient Greece to Swedish classrooms, rhetoric continues to serve as a tool for empowerment, democratic participation, and critical thinking. As a social pedagogue and a mother, I see the potential in embracing rhetoric not only as an educational subject but as a life skill that can equip individuals to become active, engaged members of society.

Anxiety and Depression in Our Young Generation

I find myself not only professionally but also personally vested in the well-being of our children. This connection runs deep and is perhaps what brings me to share with you some alarming trends about the mental health of children and teenagers in Sweden.

Since the school year of 1985/86, a national survey has been conducted every four years among fifth, seventh, and ninth graders in Sweden. This survey reveals various dimensions of health, behavior, and environments that significantly affect how our children feel.

Two specific dimensions of self-perceived symptoms have caught my attention:

1. Somatic Complaints: This includes headaches, stomach aches, backaches, and dizziness.
2. Psychological Symptoms: This consists of difficulty sleeping, feeling down, irritability, and nervousness.
   From the 2001/02 results, the data showed a growing concern, with nearly 25% of boys and 30% of girls in grade 5 reporting somatic complaints more than once a week over the last six months. By grade 9, this number had risen to 45% for girls. Psychological symptoms were even higher, affecting over 45% of boys and 50% of girls in grade 5.

Another key finding is a particular research study on stress, anxiety, and depression among 7–15-year-olds in 9 Stockholm schools. The results were unsettling; nearly one-fourth of the children felt stressed and anxious. Around 4% seemed to suffer from severe anxiety disorders, such as Generalized Anxiety Disorder (GAD) and other severe conditions.

As a mother, these findings resonate deeply with me. I find myself reflecting on the emotional well-being of my own children, especially my youngest, who is six years old. These trends make me a question: ¿How do we equip our children to handle the growing pressures they face daily?

Methods like Applied Relaxation, developed from Progressive Relaxation, have been therapeutic to reduce tension, anxiety, and worry since the early 1900s. It's heartening to know that there are practices out there that could help our children, but are we doing enough?

These rising symptoms of anxiety and depression among our children are a pressing concern that demands our collective attention. We must act now, not only as professionals and policymakers but also as parents, caregivers, teachers, and friends.

Together, let's find a way to protect and nurture the mental well-being of our children. They are, after all, our future.

My Journey to Self-love and Inclusive Education

I'd like to share my journey with you — a journey of conquering my insecurities and how they shaped my understanding and application of inclusive education as a social pedagogue in Sweden.

Embracing My True Self: A Battle Against Self-critique

As a younger woman, I grappled intensely with self-doubt and anxiety over my appearance. The mirror reflected a version of myself I found hard to love. Time, however, proved to be a wise teacher. I began to realize the energy and time I spent being frustrated and dissatisfied with myself could be better spent on acceptance and self-love.

Even as an adult, studying social pedagogy, I faced bullying for not fitting the societal norms. But the impact was different this time around; the echoes of judgment didn't shake me as they did in my childhood.

Challenges, Not Barriers: Reframing My Perspective

In my pursuit of becoming a social pedagogue, I began viewing challenges as opportunities for growth rather than barriers halting my progress. Every critique or judgment that tried to knock me down was an invitation to rise higher. We often create barriers for ourselves by judging ourselves, not loving, and accepting who we are. In essence, we restrict our own progress, our ability to evolve, to truly soar.

Through this transformation, I'm teaching my children to develop their secret weapon: self-confidence and self-esteem built on self-love. Believing in oneself fuels the engine of success, creating a strong defense against prejudice, norms, judgments, or negativity.

Unveiling the Danger of a Single Story

Recently, I came across the TED Talk by the author Chimamanda Ngozi Adichie, titled "The Danger of a Single Story". Chimamanda's words resonated deeply with me, and I was impressed by her personal experiences.

Chimamanda highlights the importance of sharing diverse narratives as educators. She defines power as "the ability not just to tell the story of another person but to make it the definitive story of that person." Her words reminded me of a particular event from my past.

Once, as a child, I visited a Romani family in my hometown, expecting to find them living in tents as per the prevailing stereotype. To my surprise, I discovered a beautiful home filled with art and craft, children with their own rooms, toys, and books — just like any other family. That day, I realized how I had unconsciously embraced a single story about the Romani people and how limiting and unjust that was.

Shaping Inclusive Narratives as a Social Pedagogue

As a social pedagogue, I believe we have a responsibility to tell all sides of stories, thereby mitigating the risk of perpetuating stereotypes and limiting knowledge. Chimamanda's video helps us see that the danger of a single story lies not in referencing another perception of facts but in questioning the legitimacy and authenticity of the story and its narrator.

I am more confident now than ever that our ideas or actions will need to be reshaped tomorrow. I want us, as future pedagogues, to understand the powerful narratives we create when working on curricula, reading lists, and assignments that govern behavioral aspects of learning, and avoid privileged narratives.

Too often, we might find ourselves repeating stereotypes about why there aren't enough women in fields such as science, technology, engineering, and mathematics. Chimamanda's story helped me realize that the role of a pedagogue is to fight against single stories because, while they can sometimes be true, they rarely provide the complete picture.

This is a call to action for us, not just as role models for future generations, but also as members of our society. Have you ever experienced the limitations of a single story? Let's broaden our understanding and share diverse narratives, together creating an inclusive and compassionate world.

How Positive Psychology and Growth Mindset Nurture Success in The Classroom

As an educator, it is both fascinating and exciting to learn about new approaches to bolster our students' well-being. One of these approaches is the concept of positive education, which I discovered through the book "Increase Well-being in School — Practical Lessons in Positive Psychology" by Åse Fagerlund. As I understand it, the aim of positive education is to develop scientifically validated positive psychological programs in school environments that enhance the well-being of both students and educators.

The school is one of the primary environments where children and youth engage in identity and social development. Hence, it becomes an ideal milieu to promote positive psychological interventions that elevate the well-being of students. The rapid growth of the positive psychology movement has resulted in its application to students of all ages. What I loved most about this concept is the integration of hope, which is central to goal-setting and achievement, essential aspects of positive psychology.

Implementing positive psychology in school environments involves helping students to set, prioritize, and clearly outline markers for what they aim to achieve. When students achieve their set goals, they can feel more accomplished and experience positive emotions, such as satisfaction. It was a significant revelation that expressing positive emotions could help them stay more focused on what will make them happier in their education and daily life, which is the foundation of positive psychology.

The test we conducted this week is part of the specific methods within positive education that focus on interventions to enhance an individual's ability to recognize their strengths and thrive, despite challenging experiences. Strength-based interventions are often employed when introducing students to positive education. I realized that using such interventions encourages individuals to utilize their character strengths in new ways. Positive psychology offers individuals ideas or tools on how to further develop their signature strengths and use them effectively.

Being open-minded and ready to learn and grow is a key aspect of education. If a student enters an educational environment with the mindset that they can improve their abilities through hard work and practice, they can be more open to new experiences and less fearful of failures. It reminded me of psychologist Carol Dweck's research into how our beliefs influence our mindset. According to Dweck, individuals can adopt a growth or a fixed mindset. These mindsets are largely based on our experiences from an early age, as the responses and opportunities we have for learning can impact how we approach new skills throughout life. While individuals with a fixed mindset believe their intellectual and personal abilities are set, a growth mindset is based on the belief that you can cultivate your intellectual ability through perseverance.

Encouraging a growth mindset means nurturing an individual's ability to develop and helping them realize they can continue to achieve beyond their current potential through hard work and persistence. Within education, a teacher's approach to praising students plays a significant role in developing students' mindsets. In her theory, Dweck explains that when teachers focused their praise on a student's intelligence (e.g., "You're so smart"), students were more likely to opt for easier tasks. In contrast, when teachers praised students for the effort they put into the task (e.g., "You worked so hard"), it motivated students to proceed to more challenging tasks. Therefore, educators must focus on praising students for the effort they put into tasks, rather than suggesting that intelligence is a fixed trait.

My Experience with the VIA Character Strengths Profile

In the pursuit of self-understanding and personal growth, we often turn to external sources of wisdom and guidance. Yet, one of the most powerful sources of insight lies within us — our character strengths. When I was studying Social Pedagogy, I had an opportunity to embark on this journey of introspection by taking the VIA Character Strengths Profile as an experiment.

Delving Deep with the VIA Character Strengths Profile

The VIA Character Strengths Profile, developed by the VIA Institute on Character, assesses an individual's unique array of strengths. In an educational setting, like the one I was in, it can serve as an excellent tool for fostering self-understanding, resilience, and empathy — all crucial skills for anyone studying Social Pedagogy.

The experiment involved taking the test, which ranks 24 character strengths under six broad virtues, and reflecting upon the results. I was intrigued and eager to discover what it would unveil about me.

My Top Five Strengths

1. Honesty (Courage)

Honesty emerged as my top strength, defining not just my truth-speaking but also the genuineness with which I present myself and take responsibility for my actions.

2. Love (Humanity)

The second strength identified was love, highlighting the value I place on close relationships, reciprocal care, and the shared bond with others.

3. Humor (Transcendence)

Humor, a strength under transcendence, is indeed something I find indispensable. It's not just about making jokes, but bringing smiles to other people's faces and seeing life's lighter side.

4. Spirituality (Transcendence)

Another significant strength for me is spirituality, reflecting my beliefs about the universe's higher purpose, my place within the larger scheme, and life's meaning.

5. Creativity (Wisdom)

Finally, creativity underscores my inclination toward novel and productive ways to conceptualize and do things. This strength extends beyond artistic pursuits, manifesting in my everyday actions and thoughts.

Sharing My Strengths: An Invitation

What initially began as an academic experiment soon turned into a profound journey of self-discovery. Seeing my character strengths laid out affirmed my understanding of myself and provided a framework to reflect upon my actions, decisions, and interactions with others.

My strengths in love, creativity, and humor manifest in my English poetry and writing. I try to infuse humor into my Instagram videos, hoping to bring a smile to those who watch them. My spirituality informs my work as a spiritual coach, guiding others on their journey of self-discovery.

When I was a Social Pedagogy student, this experiment with the VIA Character Strengths Profile was a transformative experience. It equipped me with a deeper understanding of myself and an appreciation for the power of personal strengths. Now, I extend this invitation to you: have you discovered your character strengths yet?

Embrace this journey of introspection, as we each possess a unique set of strengths that define us and guide us forward. Understanding and leveraging these strengths can be a powerful tool to enhance personal development, resilience, and happiness. The exploration begins with you.

My Journey Through Habituation and Cognitive Psychology

Life can be noisy, especially when juggling the role of a single mother and a student. When I first resumed my studies in 2019, with my little son playing nearby and the TV humming in the background, I found the noise almost unbearable. But then, something changed. This transformation, I came to realize, was habituation — a decreased response to a stimulus after repeated exposure.

Slowly, the distracting hum of the TV became nothing more than white noise, fading into the background until it barely registered in my conscious mind. This change allowed me to focus on what truly mattered: my studies and my son.

But habituation did more than just turn down the volume of life's background noise. It taught me how to trim away non-essential stimuli, helping me concentrate on tasks that required my full attention. Yet, I also learned that habituation is a fickle process, influenced by numerous factors such as the duration of exposure, and the intensity and frequency of the stimulus.

Embracing the Complexities of Parenting: There is No Perfect Formula

Perfection in parenting is a myth. As I navigated the waters of single motherhood, I learned that every child is a unique individual, deserving of respect and understanding. Just like us, they have their thoughts, values, and rights. The key to successful upbringing, I discovered, isn't about fitting our children into predefined boxes but understanding and fostering their unique talents and attributes.

I found that a blend of security, love, confidence building, and of course, a bit of fun is a great recipe for fostering my son's growth. And yes, we all have our share of traumas, big and small, which shape our adult lives. However, acknowledging and working through these traumas is an essential part of personal development.

Discovering Cognitive Psychology: How Thinking Shapes Our World

As I dove deeper into my studies, I developed a fascination for cognitive psychology, the science of how we think and how our cognition influences our behavior. I began questioning how this newfound knowledge could be applied in the classroom. Is it reliable? Is it practical to test in a learning environment? Would it improve student outcomes?

My thirst for answers led me to the article "Improving Students Learning With Effective Learning Techniques: Promising Directions From Cognitive and Educational Psychology" by Dunlosky, J., Rawson, K., Marsh, E., Nathan, M.J., and Willingham, D. (2013). Here, I learned about cognitive strategies such as testing, feedback, spacing, and interleaving and how they enhance the learning process.

Through the lens of cognitive psychology, I began to see my interactions with my son in a new light. I recognized that my constant engagement with him, encouraging him to explore his surroundings and play with his toys, was laying the groundwork for his cognitive development.

Onward: Towards a Future in Social Pedagogy

The understanding of cognitive psychology has equipped me with powerful tools to succeed as a social pedagogue. It's allowed me to foster my son's interests in Lego and mathematics and help him navigate problem-solving by offering guidance rather than solutions.

My journey through single motherhood, cognitive psychology, and my course in pedagogy has broadened my knowledge and given me the skills to build a successful future in social pedagogy. It's been a long and challenging journey, but the insights and experience gained make every step worth it.

Steering Swedish Education Through a System's Challenges and Triumphs

I would like to take you on an insightful journey about the fascinating world of Swedish education. Having spent a considerable part of my life observing, studying, and now actively participating in the Swedish education system as a Social Pedagogue, I've gained a unique perspective on the challenges and victories in our journey toward academic excellence.

In Sweden, it's a widely held belief that the direction of our schools is governed by political decisions. However, my experiences have taught me that traditions play an equally if not more significant role. This delicate balance between political mandates and traditional practices can often make school governance a complex affair.

There are multiple tools at the disposal of policymakers to exert influence over schools, such as:

- Juridical tools (laws, regulations, etc.)
- Ideological tools (educational content)
- Economic tools (budget allocations)
- Evaluative tools (checks and balances through bodies like the School Inspection)

In 1991, Swedish schools underwent decentralization, shifting responsibilities like financial management and curriculum planning to the municipalities. With this move, the influence of the state was reduced, leading to an increase in individual influence. The actors vying for control over the school system are multifaceted, ranging from political decision-makers to various organizations and community members.

The decentralization allowed local-level nuances to have a more significant impact on educational policies. This shift, while allowing for greater autonomy, also increased the challenges due to disparities in resources, demographics, and socio-economic factors among different municipalities. For example, some schools in deprived areas may struggle with staffing and providing quality education.

From my perspective as a social pedagogue, I understand the roles of school leaders and teachers better now. The vision, drive, and personality of a school's leadership, particularly the principal, significantly influence school outcomes. The quality of pedagogical methods and resources, along with demographic factors and budgets, are crucial to a school's performance.

The question we should all be asking ourselves is: What factors contribute to a school's success? What can school leaders do to ensure the best outcomes?

A 30-year retrospective on the decentralization process of Swedish schools by Fredrik Wallin touches on these very questions, highlighting issues around providing sufficient resources for students with special needs.

The dialogue around the schooling system is ever-evolving and constantly influenced by various factors, including the media and individual opinions. This system, where competition is fierce, and every decision is interlinked with budgetary considerations, could potentially see significant changes in the future.

At its core, the Swedish education system aims to blend knowledge acquisition with the cultivation of values. This blend, however, can be difficult to achieve, as focusing on one aspect often comes at the expense of the other.

In my opinion, schools need to strike a balance between academic rigor and character development. Schools should aim to facilitate students' growth into independent individuals, capable of critical thinking and decision-making. Such balance can ensure that students are not only ready for their future studies and careers but also to be responsible members of society.

In conclusion, the Swedish education system, while complex, is full of potential. As a social pedagogue, I am proud to be part of this system, and I'm excited to contribute to its growth. While there is work to be done, I am confident in our ability to continue developing, learning, and thriving in this ever-evolving landscape.

Health for Learning and Learning for Health: The Role of Social Educators

In my recent exploration of educational literature, I came across an enlightening research book titled, "Health for Learning — Learning for Health" made by the National Swedish Agency for Education. It captivated me not just because of its intriguing title, but for its extensive exploration of the significant roles schools play in children's lives. As a dedicated social educator, this book resonated with me deeply, highlighting the challenges and opportunities we face while engaging with students in our everyday practice.

Schools are pivotal in a child's life. Besides being learning hubs, they also serve as platforms for the dissemination of democratic values and the propagation of respect for human rights. This makes the role of every individual within the school premises, especially educators, exceptionally crucial. Our roles transcend teaching, encapsulating pedagogical and psychosocial aspects that collectively contribute to a student's overall development. This is what we refer to as the school's dual mission — the pedagogical and the social.

The book rightly points out, "If you feel good, it's easier to learn. But the bi-directionality also means that when you learn, it can contribute to health and well-being." It's a profound statement, one that validates my experiences as a social educator. I've noticed that when children are not in the best of spirits, they find it difficult to concentrate, perform tasks, or pay attention.

In light of the book's wisdom, it's essential to highlight Sweden's National Board of Health and Welfare's guidelines, which state, "The student health service should be used as a tool in the school's health-promoting and preventive work and in the school's work to support students' development towards the goals of education." As social educators, we are indeed critical tools for a student's well-being and development. As stated by the Swedish National Agency for Education, we should work towards developing good relations and social skills among students, thereby strengthening their self-esteem and resilience.

However, the journey to accomplishing this task is not solitary. It calls for a harmonious collaboration between social educators and the student health team. The objective is clear — to support students optimally. Transparency, good communication, and a well-structured approach are essential elements of this process. We must work towards understanding each student's unique situation and the underlying reasons for their problems. With patience and empathy, we can build trust and understanding, forming the basis for effective measures to facilitate their return to school.

Other entities like child and adolescent psychiatry, youth centers, social services, and police can also lend support to the school's efforts. Despite this, the school still holds the primary responsibility for students, particularly in areas of its competence.

In conclusion, the role of the social pedagogue, like myself, is instrumental in promoting an environment conducive to learning and overall health. Our actions should aim at ensuring that student health services are visible, accessible, and responsive to students' needs. Whether it's through mandatory meetings with the school counselor or increased communication with other school staff, every step we take brings us closer to creating a meaningful school experience for every student.

Creating a Culture of Equality Through Equality Action Plans in School

I wish to share with you some thoughts and reflections that have been occupying my mind over the past couple of weeks. My focus has been on the topic of Equality Action Plans, an essential tool in the education sector that sets the tone for an inclusive, welcoming, and fair learning environment.

In my quest to understand these plans better, I have been studying the ones implemented in various high schools, with one particular school standing out. For the sake of confidentiality, let's refer to this institution as Enigma School.

The Equality Action Plan at Enigma School is truly intriguing. According to the plan, the school staff takes a firm stand against any form of offensive treatment, discrimination, or harassment. The institution has adopted a zero-tolerance policy, running ongoing training programs to ensure that this policy is upheld. The ultimate goal? To create a school environment where students feel safe, where comfort and security are assured.

This plan, set by the school management, is revisited annually to ensure it continues to serve its purpose. Transparency is key — the plan is readily accessible to students and guardians alike, and the implemented strategies are evaluated annually for effectiveness.

The Enigma School Equality Action Plan comprises numerous innovative strategies. For instance, they organize outdoor days for all students at the beginning and end of the academic year. The aim is to strengthen social cohesion among students through activities like volleyball, cooperative exercises, walks, and quiz walks.

One of the impactful interventions has been the Motivational Boost, an educational program for all school staff coordinated by the Central Student Health through the Star for Life's auspices.

An additional initiative, known as Mindset, was conducted by a social worker and a school psychologist from Central Student Health. The duo visited first-year classes and conducted lessons on the concept of mindset.

The Student Council plays an integral role in the Equality Action Plan, enhancing the school's culture by influencing different events like the Lucia procession, school entertainment, and discussions around LGBTQI, discrimination, and offensive treatment.

The plan also includes a special study day with themes such as anti-Semitism for school staff, consisting of lectures/workshops conducted by coordinators against anti-Semitism. Follow-ups are done through peer learning and general staff meetings.

Psychosocial surveys concerning the use of harsh language at school are part of the plan, providing insights through individual student interviews. This helps to improve the study environment in classrooms.

The school nurse can share de-identified information about group/class health based on health conversations, contributing to the plan's holistic approach.

The Equality Action Plan actively involves the student body by informing them about the student council, conducting group discussions, collaborating with the library on literature, and creating posters on equality.

Changing Attitudes, Shaping Identities: The Power of Role Models and Inclusive Narratives

I will share my experiences and some of the lessons I've learned in my journey toward fostering inclusivity and compassion.

The Obama Effect: Altering Attitudes and Prejudices

In the realm of changing attitudes, a study that I found particularly impactful is captured in the book "The Obama Effect. How the 2008 Campaign Changed White Racial Attitudes" by Seth K. Goldman and Diana C. Mutzis. This insightful book brings to light a trend of diminished racial prejudice among white Americans toward Black people during Barack Obama's presidential campaign in 2008.

Interestingly, Obama's media prominence during this period unintentionally served to challenge negative racial stereotypes among white Americans. But this attitude shift was sadly short-lived. By 2010, racial prejudices among whites had largely reverted to pre-2008 levels, which Goldman and Mutzis attribute to a significant decline in media coverage of Obama, allowing negative stereotypes to resurface.

The authors conclude two significant things: racial attitudes can change even within short periods, and the portrayal of Afro-Americans in mass media significantly influences these changes.

Single Parents: An Untold Story of Strength

Further exploring the strength of non-traditional family structures, I was drawn to Bella dePaulo's work, "Single Parents and Their Children: The Good News No One Ever Tells You".

Bella dePaulo argues that single parents spending quality time with their children can cultivate a unique bond that could potentially be stronger than in two-parent families.

Moreover Bella dePaulo's article titled, "The Children of Single Parents Are Doing Better Than You Realized" dissects common misconceptions and highlights the resilience of single-parent families. The main challenge they face is economic, not emotional.

Indeed, societal support should focus on how to improve the living conditions of these families rather than stigmatizing their family situation.

Humor, Gender Identity, and Peer Pressure

Diving into the depths of gender identity, I find humor plays a complex role. Sigmund Freud's "Jokes and Their Relation to the Unconscious" highlights how humor can either lead to acceptance or exclusion in a group setting.

In the context of developing gender identities, humor can sometimes result in the creation of social distances. For instance, my sons, influenced by peer pressure and societal norms, used to make jokes they didn't fully understand, just to fit in with their peers. It's a poignant reminder of the relevance of this subject to parents, educators, and mental health professionals alike.

Freud outlines how an individual is often coerced to choose between laughing at offensive jokes or taking a stand, a choice that can lead to ostracization or a denial of their own gender identity.

A Call for Change: Equality and Respect

As a social pedagogue, I am committed to the fight against discrimination, harassment, and unfair treatment rooted in societal norms. The journey begins with nurturing respect for diverse narratives and fostering inclusive education that challenges stereotypes.

Let's redefine family structures, challenge norms, and encourage one another on this journey toward a more inclusive and compassionate world.

Social Learning Theory: Rewards, Punishments, and the Importance of Setting Boundaries

I have been deeply engrossed in the book "Psychology: Science or Madness?" by Mikael Lundgren and found myself reflecting on the chapter about learning psychology, specifically the concepts of rewards and punishments. The book proposes that behavior will continue if it is rewarded and cease if it is punished.

However, I began contemplating the concept of punishment. In some cases, it might be perceived as a reward, thus losing its intended purpose. Consider a child who exhibits an undesired behavior — they are typically admonished, possibly sent to their room, or asked to leave the classroom. However, these actions don't always lead to the cessation of the behavior. In some instances, the behavior escalates. The child is getting a reaction to their actions, even if it's negative, and this in itself may be received as a reward, thus prompting continued and possibly escalated behavior.

In such scenarios, I believe it's crucial not to stop at the punishment phase, that is, telling the child they have done wrong and leaving it at that. It's of utmost importance to explain, discuss, and collectively reflect on what went wrong and what could have been done differently.

As a single parent and a future social pedagogue, I prefer to use the terms encouragement and praise rather than rewards, and setting boundaries instead of punishment. Clear boundaries are essential in a child's upbringing, teaching them social skills, moral values, and ethical principles. An example is the "Stop! My body!" learning method used in preschools to prevent unwanted physical contact. Is about very simple, but fundamental body rules:

1. YOU HAVE CONTROL OVER YOUR OWN BODY and others have control over their bodies.
2. You decide who can hug and kiss you, or do something with your body.
3. No one is allowed to touch your PRIVATE PARTS in a way that you do not understand. Sometimes adults, such as parents or a doctor, may need to do so, but they should then explain to you what they are doing and why.
4. No one is allowed to force you to touch your private parts, nor touch someone else's.
5. No one is allowed to photograph or film your private parts. No one may share or distribute such images.

As an adult and a parent, I appreciate this approach and apply it in my daily life.

Praising and encouraging a child is also essential for their understanding that their hard work is valued, and they are valued.

Doing so enhances their self-confidence and self-esteem. However, the most important lesson is that actions have consequences, either good or bad, depending on what and how one does it.

The book "Psychology: Science or Madness?" explores Albert Bandura's social learning theory. The Canadian psychologist posits that humans observe, imitate, and develop in specific social environments, with certain mental states promoting or hindering learning. This reminds me of Vygotsky, as both theorists incorporate a social element into learning and assert that humans can acquire new knowledge and behaviors by observing others. This phenomenon, known as observational learning, can be used to explain various behaviors, including those often unexplained by other learning theories.

One event that deeply resonated with me was Bandura's 1961 Bobo doll experiment. In the experiment, an adult displayed either gentle or aggressive behavior toward a doll in front of a group of children. The children who observed the gentle behavior mimicked it, while those who witnessed the aggressive behavior also replicated it.

This takes me back to when my son was 1.5 years old and attended daycare. There was an older child, almost three, who was frequently aggressive and angry. During discussions at the principal's office, I noticed the child's parents quarreling with each other, the father being particularly frustrated and upset. It dawned on me that the child was merely imitating the behavior of his closest adult figures. As adults, we often forget that we serve as role models to our children every day. It's crucial to be mindful of our behavior, especially during their formative years.

As a social pedagogue, I believe that mastering social learning theory is a must since we become the adults that children observe and possibly imitate. By possessing strong moral, ethical, and social values, and pedagogical knowledge, this challenge becomes much easier.

As a parent, I take immense pride in being a good example to my children. I feel joy and immense gratitude as I continue to grow and improve every day.

The Rhythm of Sleep: A Insight into Youth Sleep Habits

I find the subject of sleep profoundly significant in the development of children and adolescents. From my professional work with children with NDD (Neurodevelopmental Disorders) to my daily experience as a parent, the importance of sleep in nurturing mental and physical well-being resonates deeply with me.

The Essence of Sleep: More than Just Rest

Sleep is not merely a biological necessity but an integral part of human existence. The calming descent into slumber allows the body to regenerate, lowering blood pressure, pulse, and body temperature. Muscles relax, brain activity reduces, and the immune system gets activated (Bengtsson 2013; Hillman 2012, ss.17,18). Hormones like melatonin guide the body's rhythm, playing a crucial role in our ability to fall asleep and wake up refreshed.

What is less talked about is the rhythm and balance that sleep creates within our bodies. It's not just about physical rest but aligning the natural rhythms that allow us to maintain a sense of balance and well-being (Dahlberg & Segersten 2010, ss. 65–69). A sound sleep lends strength to the day ahead and fosters resilience against stress and illness (Hillman 2012, ss.17,18).

The Sleep Crisis Among Youth

The youth, particularly teenagers, face unique challenges in maintaining healthy sleep patterns. With the introduction of new technologies and changing lifestyles, sleep disturbances have become alarmingly prevalent. Today, 33% of 10–18-year-olds have difficulty falling asleep, and 61% report feeling tired during school at least once a week (Socialstyrelsen 2014, s. 114).

The consequences are not to be taken lightly. From difficulties in problem-solving and increased stress sensitivity to long-term effects like obesity and diabetes, sleep deprivation takes a toll (Hillman 2012, ss.21–23).

Addressing the Challenge: A Social Pedagogue's Role

In my role as a social pedagogue, I recognize the importance of approaching sleep issues holistically. The new term "elevhälsan" (pupil health), introduced in 2011, emphasizes the need for medical, psychosocial, special education, and psychological interventions (Skolverket 2013, s.1). This is where the role of school nurses and social pedagogues becomes central.

We need to catch sleep problems early, provide guidance, and follow up with support (Socialstyrelsen 2014, ss.15,35). We have the potential to make a significant impact on public health through proper sleep education and intervention in schools (Mayumi, et al. 2012, s.177).

A Personal Note

As a mother, I see my children's sleep as a precious commodity. As a professional, I understand the science and social constructs that govern it. Let's join hands in ensuring our children get the rest they need, recognizing sleep as a rhythm that fuels life.

By sincerely bridging the personal with the professional, I hope to have reached out to your hearts, dear readers. Sleep well, for it is not just a necessity but a melody that plays the tune of our lives.

Understanding Academic Stress Among Swedish Adolescents

My interest in the well-being of children, especially those dealing with the immense pressures of school life, has been a continuous journey. Coupled with my experience working with children diagnosed with NDD, this exploration is not just professional but deeply personal.

In Sweden, unlike the abundance of studies in the U.S., research on adolescent well-being is relatively scarce. The unique challenges faced by Swedish ninth-graders, including numerous future choices and the pressure to perform well in final grades, have stirred my curiosity and concern. Here, I hope to shed light on some crucial findings that affect our children's mental and physical health.

1. Stress in School Life: A Growing Concern

According to a survey conducted by Skolverket in 2012, 26% of students in grades 7–9 often or always felt stressed at school. The primary stress factors were homework, tests, grades, and self-imposed demands (Skolverket, 2013). Another study by Nygren, Janlert, and Nygren (2011) analyzed various factors contributing to the well-being of Swedish adolescents in grades 7–9. The results were alarming: 51% of young men and 65% of young women felt stressed about school once a week or more often.

2. Stress and Health: The Unseen Damage

Stress is no stranger to negative implications on an individual's mental, somatic, and physical health. Both frequent daily stressors and significant negative life events have been found to correlate with deteriorated general health (DeLongis et al., 1982; Holahan & Moon, 1990; Segerstrom & Miller, 2004). High school students often experience both short-term stressors, such as exams, and long-term stressors like working towards final grades and waiting for admissions results.

3. The Role of Self-Efficacy in Adolescence

The concept of self-efficacy, or an individual's belief in their ability to manage various situations, is crucial during adolescence. This belief system develops dramatically during this phase and particularly in puberty. Students with low self-efficacy are more susceptible to academic anxiety, whereas higher self-efficacy correlates with higher school belonging and lessen symptoms of anxiety and depression (Bandura, 1997; Moeini et al., 2008; Muris et al., 2001).

4. Coping Strategies: Problem-Focused vs. Emotion-Focused

Coping mechanisms, whether problem-focused (changing the situation) or emotion-focused (regulating emotions), play a vital role in managing stress. Which strategy to use depends on context, the individuals involved, and the individual's assessment of the situation (Lazarus & Folkman, 1980; 1984; Folkman et al., 1986). This assessment often ties back to self-efficacy, emphasizing its importance in shaping our response to stress.

Final Thoughts

As parents, educators, and social pedagogues, it's our shared responsibility to understand the stress and challenges our children face. The findings from these Swedish studies pave the way for targeted interventions that not only identify but address the underlying variables of academic stress. By understanding the interactions between stress, self-efficacy, and coping strategies, we can equip our children with the tools they need to thrive in school and beyond.

Unlocking the Power of Cognitive Behavioral Therapy (CBT)

Parenting and NDD Care

I often find myself at the intersection of professional knowledge and personal experience, especially in my work with children diagnosed with NDD (Neurodevelopmental Disorders). In the fascinating world of cognitive behavioral therapy (CBT), I have discovered a rich tapestry of approaches that resonate with my dual role.

Understanding CBT: Beyond the Textbook

CBT, based on research in learning psychology, cognitive psychology, and social psychology, focuses on the interplay between environment and individual. It emphasizes here-and-now interactions. The term "behavior" in CBT refers to various physical reactions, interpretations, specific actions, and perceptions of events that influence both the person and the surroundings.

The Individualized Approach: A Social Pedagogue's Touch

CBT practitioners conduct a highly individualized behavior analysis to understand the interaction between a person and their environment. Whether in a group or individual setting, this approach has proven highly effective in treating psychological problems. As a social pedagogue, I appreciate this personalized touch, emphasizing the uniqueness of every individual.

A Constant Evolution: Adapting and Growing

Lundh (2006) highlights that CBT is continually evolving, responding to new research findings. There's no binding ideology, which enables CBT to adapt to fresh insights. This dynamism aligns with the social pedagogy principle of fostering growth and development within the social context.

Collaboration and Empowerment: CBT's Core Strengths

Kåver (2006) emphasizes CBT's collaborative nature. The therapist and patient work together, not only in sessions but also through homework assignments. This cooperative approach echoes the social pedagogue's belief in empowering individuals to take charge of their lives.

Humanistic Values and the Holistic Approach

CBT's roots in humanism, with a focus on well-being, resonate with the broader principles of social pedagogy. The therapy's emphasis on enhancing what works well, rather than merely fixing what's wrong, aligns with a social pedagogue's desire to see the whole person.

Behavioral Concerns in Children: A Parent's Perspective

As a mother, I find comfort in Webster-Stratton's (2004) assertion that behavioral issues in children are normal. CBT's techniques to manage and gradually improve behavior, even in energetic children, are reassuring. It's about guiding the child, not suppressing them.

Social Integration in Learning: The Classroom Context

Evenshaug & Hallen (2001) illustrate the connection between social acceptance and academic performance. This reflects the social pedagogue's focus on creating a nurturing learning environment. Self-image, self-esteem, and a strong foundation from the family play a crucial role in learning and development.

Bridging Theories and Practices

My journey through CBT has been a process of connecting theoretical knowledge with practical experience. The blend of social pedagogy principles and personal insights as a mother provides a unique perspective on the multifaceted nature of CBT.

CBT's humanistic values, individualized approach, continuous evolution, and focus on collaboration align beautifully with my beliefs as a social pedagogue. It's not merely a therapy form; it's a philosophy that helps both my children and the children I work with, especially those with NDD, to blossom.

With love and understanding, I share these insights with you, dear readers. Whether you're a parent, educator, or therapist, may you find inspiration and guidance in the beautiful synergy between CBT and social pedagogy.

The PAX Method in Swedish Schools: A Critical Look

In my professional life, I've had the opportunity to work with children with different needs, including those diagnosed with Neurodevelopmental Disorders (NDD). Today, I want to share with you my personal and heartfelt reflections on a method that has been gaining traction in many Swedish schools: PAX.

PAX, a manual-based classroom method aimed at creating calm in the classroom, is heralded by some as a remarkable solution. But there are facets that concern me deeply, both as a professional in the field and as a parent. I've taken the time to critically review this method and wish to share my findings and personal thoughts with you.

PAX in Schools: A Brief Overview

PAX in school is the Swedish adaptation of the Good Behavior Game, an American method rooted in applied behavior analysis. It focuses on reinforcements rather than aversive elements like punishment. But is the absence of a reward really any different from a punishment?

In PAX, students are divided into groups, and all members must behave well for a fixed period to participate in a fun class activity. Those who disrupt don't get the reward, while others enjoy it. This can lead to what children I have spoken with described as collective punishment, something not allowed in Swedish schools according to Skolverket (Swedish National Agency for Education).

Critical Concerns about PAX: Does PAX Work in School?

PAX has been shown to make classrooms quieter and students more obedient. But obedience is not an educational goal in Sweden. Rather, schools should foster independence, something that conflicts with PAX's obedience-driven approach. We must ask ourselves whether we want obedience to be a key focus in our schools.

Does PAX Work for Everyone?

The method doesn't consider children with functional disabilities. Rewarding students without disabilities for achievements that children with disabilities like ADHD or autism cannot attain is discrimination. At least 5% of Swedish primary school students have an ADHD diagnosis, and at least 1% have an autism diagnosis. PAX, in this sense, systematically discriminates against these students.

What about Different Ages?

The effectiveness of PAX differs across age groups. It may work in lower grades but fails in higher grades, where teenagers are striving for independence. A similar method, PALS, faced similar challenges in Danish schools. Also, there's evidence that methods like PAX may lead to low self-esteem in the long run.

Consent Issues

My greatest concern with PAX is the absence of informed consent. In any intervention, psychologists are required to work with the consent of those affected. PAX doesn't offer this choice. This contradicts the way psychologists usually work and the ethical principles they adhere to.

Final Thoughts

PAX in Swedish schools may have some immediate benefits in creating a quieter classroom environment, but the long-term implications and ethical considerations must not be overlooked. As a social pedagogue and a mother, I urge educators, psychologists, and parents to critically assess this method, considering the individual needs of our children and the principles of our education system.

As we strive to create nurturing and inclusive classrooms, let's remember that there's no one-size-fits-all solution. Each child's individuality, dignity, and rights must be our guiding principles.

Motivational Interviewing in Education

I have discovered an inspiring and successful method for nurturing motivation in working with children, especially those with diagnoses like NDD (Neurodevelopmental Disorders). This method, known as Motivational Interviewing (MI), was developed in the '80s and has evolved and gained traction across various educational contexts. I would like to share insights into how MI can be used in schools to increase both students' and educators' motivation.

1. Understanding Motivational Interviewing (MI)

MI is essentially a conversation-based method to foster a person's intrinsic motivation to change problematic behaviors. It's about awakening an individual's inherent will to change by amplifying their natural drive (Ortiz, 2010). Instead of coercing or imposing change, the method emphasizes collaboration between the leader and the participant, with empathy and mutual trust at the core.

Farbring and Rollnick (2015) describe MI as a scientifically grounded tool for enhancing an individual's intrinsic motivation, and guiding them toward change. Barth and Näsholm (2006) believe it opens avenues for reflection, considering the individual as competent and capable of decision-making. By emphasizing inner dialogues and personal thoughts, MI promotes development through conversation.

2. Implementing MI in Schools

MI has emerged as a powerful tool within educational environments to motivate both students and pedagogues (Blom & Rose, 2007). It has been particularly effective among students with problematic school attendance or low study motivation.

Positive Impact on Students

Holm Ivarsson (2013) found MI to be a directive method, shaping the conversation to highlight positive aspects leading to change. It fosters the student's autonomy and motivation, strengthening their self-determination and control (Rollnick et al., 2017). MI is seen as empathetic and understanding of the participant's situation (Eriksson, 2016).

Challenges and Limitations

Although there's limited research on MI about learning, many argue that it is a potent method for boosting student motivation (Frey et al., 2011; Cryer & Atkinson, 2015). Motivation is often seen as complex and multifaceted, driven by both internal and external factors (Giota, 2006). Striking the right balance between these aspects can be challenging.

3. MI, Education, and Research

Studies like that by Terry (2016) highlight the potential of MI to foster a sense of motivation and engagement, enhancing cognitive skills and goal fulfillment. Blom and Rose (2007) emphasize MI as a constructive way to develop an individual's inner motivation for change. Empathy is central to success in this model, per Feller and Cottone (2003).

A Personal Reflection as a Parent and Pedagogue

In my own experiences, both as a mother and a social pedagogue working with children with NDD, I've seen the transformative power of MI. By connecting with the child's interests, desires, and autonomy, MI encourages growth and builds a foundation for lifelong learning.

Motivational Interviewing in education is not merely a method; it's a compassionate approach that recognizes the student's individuality, fosters positive relationships, and empowers change.

Unlocking Potential With a Compassionate Approach to Learning

I understand the complex dynamics of motivation in learning and have observed how different motivational factors can shape the learning experience for children.

One of the remarkable concepts that has caught my attention over the years is Self-Determination Theory (SDT). This theory, developed by Richard M. Ryan and Edward L. Deci, speaks to the heart of what many educators strive for — fostering a love of learning that comes from within the student.

Embracing Intrinsic Motivation

Twenty years ago, Ryan and Deci introduced their thoughts on intrinsic and extrinsic motivation. Fast forward to today, their Self-Determination Theory has evolved to become a crucial aspect of pedagogy, focusing on the intrinsic factors that encourage students to learn, grow, and thrive.

According to SDT, humans naturally want to grow, learn, and develop. In the educational context, it means that students inherently possess the motivation to learn, but this internal drive often dwindles over time, obscured by external pressures and an often controlling educational environment.

Three Pillars of Self-Determination

Self-determination theory highlights three basic needs that lead to intrinsic motivation:

1. Autonomy: Students must feel a sense of independence, able to take initiative, and experience psychological freedom in their learning process.
2. Competence: The need to feel capable, believing that their learning process will result in achieving their goals.
3. Community: Positive, mutual relationships built on trust and closeness that foster a sense of belonging.

The Role of Teachers

One essential factor in nurturing these three needs is the engagement of teachers. A supportive, structured, and warm motivational style, rather than a controlling and cold one, significantly impacts the students' intrinsic motivation.

Studies have shown that external rewards, punishments, and excessive testing can have harmful effects on motivation and learning. Instead, positive feedback, empathy, clear goals, and choice lead to intrinsic motivation, which subsequently fosters lifelong learning rather than mere test preparation.

A Holistic Approach

It's not just the classroom teacher that contributes to this elevated motivation. The school itself must create a motivating climate for both teachers and students. If teachers feel autonomous, competent, and part of a social community, they can instill the same values in their students.

Using Self-Determination Theory in learning environments can satisfy these fundamental needs, fostering a motivating school climate that benefits all students.

Learning for Life

As we journey through the educational landscape, embracing theories like SDT can make a profound difference. Speaking both as a Social Pedagogue and a mother, I can attest to the transformational power of intrinsic motivation in shaping our children's future. Let's guide our students not just toward passing the next test but toward learning for life.

Social Pedagogy and Personal Growth in a Multicultural World

As a single parent, my life is a complex weaving of roles and responsibilities. Each day brings a blend of unique experiences and challenges. Navigating through the realms of social constructivism and multicultural societies, I find myself sailing in uncharted waters, with my child's future as my guiding star.

From my professional standpoint as a social pedagogue, society and its contexts are a rich tapestry of learning opportunities. The thought of engaging a classroom or a family room filled with diverse interests can be overwhelming, yet fascinating. Instead of striving to forge a common interest, I've learned that harnessing the power of individual curiosity can lead to profound growth and understanding.

For instance, curiosity recently led me down the path of music. Even with no inherent interest or skill, I found myself yearning to create harmony with my voice and a guitar. Countless hours of practice later, my voice now carries a tune, and my fingers are slowly finding their rhythm on the guitar strings. It's a testament to the power of hard work, patience, and practice — the symphony of growth.

As I delve deeper into the world of social pedagogy, I am often captivated by the ideas of German philosopher and educator, Paul Natorp. His triadic vision of the individual, society, and education rings true as I consider the upbringing of my child in our increasingly multicultural world.

Once, the family was the primary care unit, supporting children, the elderly, and the sick, reflective of a conservative welfare state. But now, in our social-democratic Nordic societies, (I live in Sweden) the state works hand in hand with families like mine to shoulder this responsibility. It's a step forward, yet the question arises: where does community fit into modern social pedagogy?

In the intricate dance of life, I believe that while community remains vital, it isn't the central star around which everything else orbits. Rather, it's become one of the many celestial bodies in the vast expanse of social education. It is significant, but not solitary.

In contemporary education, the child, as an individual, is at the core. Italian educator Loris Malaguzzi's philosophy resonates with me as I guide my little boy through life's maze. Malaguzzi believed in the infinite curiosity and potential nestled within each child. A belief I see embodied in my son every day. He isn't a passive receiver; he's an active participant in his learning journey.

Through Malaguzzi's lens, my son isn't just a child; he's a co-creator of knowledge, building relationships, and making sense of his world. His contribution to his life journey and the broader human experience is invaluable.

As I empower my son to engage in everyday tasks like planning meals or vacations, I see his confidence bloom. His eyes sparkle with the realization that he's capable, important, and an active participant in life's grand adventure.

His world expands through play, where he's most receptive and open to learning, whether he's crafting castles with building blocks or role-playing as a superhero. As his mother, I'm his biggest cheerleader, equally enthralled in our adventures, be it in our imaginary castle or our little kitchen.

The complexities of social pedagogy, multiculturalism, and individual development can be overwhelming. However, as a single parent and social pedagogue, I've realized that embracing these intricacies can lead to enriching experiences for my child and myself. It's about striking a balance between recognizing the individual and the community, appreciating our diverse society, and creating a space where curiosity can blossom.

It's in the struggle, growth, and triumphs of this journey that I truly understand the profound beauty and potential of social pedagogy. And it's a journey I'm honored to take, hand-in-hand with my child, as we learn and grow together, each day, one song at a time.

The Unique Journey to Combat Student Absenteeism

A personal reflection on the enhanced individual alternative schooling method

Let me take you on a journey to a unique school I recently visited, an institution that's courageously paving a new path in education. This institution, which we'll refer to as "Odyssey House," is part of an acclaimed city rich in educational and cultural diversity. The most remarkable thing about Odyssey House is its specific focus on a program called the "Enhanced Individual Alternative".

This innovative model aims to help students who struggle with regular school attendance, working relentlessly to reintegrate them back into the school system. Each student in this program has an individual study plan and a personal schedule that evolves gradually according to their progress. This meticulous planning ensures that students always have access to their daily plans at their workstations, providing a structure that's both flexible and accommodating.

Upon my visit, I had the privilege of meeting various staff members, including mentors, subject teachers, student assistants, and social pedagogues. These passionate educators work in harmony within a calm, homely environment, customizing their pedagogy to fit each student's unique needs. This personalized approach considers students' varied capabilities, greatly enhancing their learning experience.

Odyssey House offers a total of 18 student spots, implying a small teacher-student ratio that allows for a more personalized learning environment. Furthermore, they maintain a close collaboration with external professionals in the student's network, such as the National Center for Psychiatric Support and Treatment for Children and Young People, The Swedish Act concerning Support and Service for Persons with Certain Functional Impairments, and Social Services, ensuring a holistic approach to each student's development.

Their system operates based on a unique step-by-step model that is continuously being evaluated and updated. The first meeting with the student and the guardian takes place either at Odyssey House or at a location of their choice. The creation of an individual schedule occurs in harmony with the student, their guardian, and their network, taking into consideration the student's personal interests and functional needs.

The approach to waking and fetching the student from school is as individualized as their learning plan, showing their unwavering commitment to meeting each student's unique needs. The faculty collaborates with the student, their guardian, and their network to understand any existing functional impairments and how these may affect the student's learning and daily life.

The school adapts its schedule according to the student's needs, which means that initially, they may have shorter school days. The teaching is individualized, based on each student's study plan and personal schedule. They work based on the learning strategies the student possesses, refining them over time to improve their study techniques.

Once a student's attendance stabilizes, the staff collaboratively decides on the best way to extend their school day. This could include introducing more subjects, for instance. The schedule expands, and school days become longer.

Contact with parents and guardians is vital to their practice and is enhanced through different evening arrangements, such as drop-in coffee sessions for new and "old" parents. Conversations about the student's next steps after Odyssey House begin, considering options such as the Enhanced Program, National Program, High School, or internships at adapted workplaces.

The smooth transition from Odyssey House to the new school or workplace is facilitated by the staff through various measures like trial days, network meetings, visits to the new school, and handover conversations with the new school's personnel.

Upon completion of their time at Odyssey House, students are integrated into their new activity while the staff evaluates their time at Odyssey House through surveys and continuous follow-ups.

In a world where the traditional education system often fails to accommodate the needs of all students, Odyssey House represents a beacon of hope for students who struggle with regular attendance. Its unique approach highlights the importance of individualized learning and support, offering a more inclusive education solution.

The Power of Low-Affect in Education

Sweden's classrooms have seen an evolution in recent years. As a reader of Maria Bühler, Annelie Karlsson, and Terése Österholm's enlightening book "Low-Affect Approach and Problematic School Absence," I've found myself inspired and better equipped to tackle the challenges of my professional life. This book delves into how understanding problematic school absenteeism through a low-affect approach can foster a more conducive environment for students to remain engaged and present at school.

From my early experiences in Sweden's educational system to my current role, one reality has stood clear: a welcoming, supportive environment is crucial for students. The 2018 publication "10 Reasons for Dropout" by the Agency for Youth and Civil Society Affairs asserts that bullying and a lack of pedagogical support are leading causes of high school dropout. These factors combined can lead to a heightened level of mental health issues among students, further impacting their academic performance.

As an advocate of every child's right to education, as mandated by the Swedish School Law (School Regulation 2010:800) and the UN Convention on the Rights of the Child, I believe in the significance of regular attendance. My philosophy aligns with the Convention's stance that educational institutions, municipalities, and county councils should encourage regular attendance and reduce study disruptions.

One invaluable concept I've learned and shared in my digital meetings is KASAM — the sense of coherence. This concept, coined by Professor Aaron Antonovsky in 1991, is incredibly pertinent when discussing problematic school absenteeism. It comprises three components: comprehensibility, manageability, and meaningfulness.

I remember instances from my school days when students stayed home due to various circumstances, including troubled home situations, mental health issues, or bullying. Today, the number of students staying home has dramatically increased. Schools and authorities were not prepared for this surge. To tackle this issue, more training courses on managing problematic school absenteeism have been offered, even in the summer, at various educational institutions.

As a participant in these courses, I am grateful for the wealth of knowledge and information that I can apply to my role. The key is to truly understand and get to know the students. Working closely with children and young people gives us the unique opportunity to build trust and assist them in the best way possible, in alignment with school laws and the Children's Convention. By understanding their needs, we can create a more comprehensible, manageable, and meaningful schooling experience for them.

The book mentions, "Parents need to be able to go to their jobs, and schools need to solve the problems that arise in the school environment" (p. 30). As social educators, it is vital for us to work proactively to reduce school absenteeism.

The Power of Roles and Moral Reasoning

Group conformity, power dynamics, and the stages of moral development

During my studies in Social Pedagogy, a particular lecture sparked my curiosity about roles, more specifically about groupthink and how groups behave. To deepen my understanding, I turned to the book Psychology — Science or Madness? This led me to delve into the intriguing and sometimes chilling realm of psychological experiments and theories.

Social Pedagogy is an interdisciplinary approach that combines education, social work, and psychology to support children's holistic development. It emphasizes the importance of relationships, participation, and empowerment in learning.

It focuses on nurturing the well-being of children and promoting their social, emotional, and cognitive growth. It aims to create inclusive and supportive environments where they can actively engage, learn, and develop their potential.

The Roles We Play: Bandura and Zimbardo

In a 1975 experiment conducted by psychologist Albert Bandura, college students were informed that they would be working with students from another school on a group task.

In one scenario, they overheard an assistant labeling the other students as "animals," while in another, the assistant referred to them as "nice." Bandura discovered that the students were more likely to administer what they believed were increasing levels of electric shocks to the other students if they had heard them referred to as "animals."

Reflecting on this experiment, I considered the concept of power and group conformity. The Stanford Prison Experiment conducted by Philip Zimbardo in 1970 came to my mind. It is vividly depicted in the 2010 movie "The Experiment," featuring Adrien Brody and Forest Whitaker.

The experiment demonstrated how it's easier for people to reduce their sense of personal responsibility when others can't identify them, allowing individuals to hide behind a uniform or a role.

The Stanford Prison Experiment involved 24 university students playing the roles of either prisoners or guards. Within just six days, the 'guards' started demonstrating brutal and offensive behavior towards the 'prisoners,' leading Zimbardo to end the experiment prematurely.

The study revealed how institutional forces and group pressure could make ordinary volunteers ignore the potential harm their actions might cause to others.

Moral Development: Lawrence Kohlberg's Model

While studying, I also learned about the cognitive model of moral development as proposed by Lawrence Kohlberg. Building on Jean Piaget's idea of moral development occurring in stages based on life experiences and active reasoning, Kohlberg expanded this by studying how moral reasoning changes as we grow up.

Kohlberg's model is divided into three levels — Pre-conventional, Conventional, and Post-conventional — each containing two stages. These stages help explain how people determine right from wrong and how our moral reasoning evolves as we mature.

From a Social Pedagogy perspective, I found Kohlberg's model of moral development to be an invaluable tool for understanding students' moral progression at different stages. It provides a framework for creating an effective learning environment where rules, rewards, and group dynamics are all leveraged to facilitate the moral growth of students.

Moral Reasoning: A Personal Perspective

The book presents a thought-provoking example involving a man whose wife is dying from cancer. A scientist has developed a drug but is selling it at an exorbitant price. The husband manages to gather only half the amount, and the researcher refuses to lower the price. Driven by desperation, the man breaks into the laboratory and steals the drug to save his wife.

In this moral dilemma, I empathize with the man's actions. I believe that the value of life far outweighs the value of money. However, I also recognize, as per Martin Hoffman's perspective, that moral behavior is fundamentally rooted in empathy. Therefore, if faced with a similar situation, I would not hesitate to break the law to save my loved ones.

The Pursuit of Knowledge and the Quest for Right Actions

As I continue to explore the vast realms of Social Pedagogy and Psychology, I understand the importance of questioning continuously and seeking knowledge from various credible sources. Even when information comes from authority figures, it's each person's responsibility to critically evaluate it before making a decision.

As I look forward to learning more about psychology, my ultimate goal is to use this knowledge to perform my role as a social pedagogue more effectively. We all play various roles in life, and understanding the psychology behind our behaviors can significantly improve how we navigate these roles and make moral decisions.

Exploring Low-Arousal Approach for Children with Autism and ADHD

In my exploration of "Autism and ADHD in High School Part 2" by David Edfelt, Annelie Karlsson, Ann Lindgren, and Anna Sjölund, I came across the concept of clarifying pedagogy, which aims to make events, actions, and environments comprehensible, manageable, and meaningful which I apply in my work as well. This pedagogy revolves around answering key questions:

- What am I supposed to do?
- Where should I be?
- When should I do it?
- With whom?
- How long/how much?
- When does it end?
- What should I do next?

For an autistic child who may struggle to understand language, these questions can be addressed using visuals, symbols, colors, numbers, or objects. Conversely, an autistic child who comprehends language well may thrive with written lists of tasks and labels.

One notable approach in this domain is the TEACCH method (Treatment and Education of Autistic and Communication Handicapped Children). It is specifically designed for individuals on the autism spectrum, taking into account the characteristic traits of autism and the unique difficulties faced by each child. TEACCH employs structured and continuous interventions, environmental adaptations, and alternative communication training. It can also be combined with other approaches or therapies. Developed by Dr. Eric Schopler and Dr. Robert Reichler at the University of North Carolina in the 1960s, this methodology offers a structured form of visual learning known as clarifying pedagogy in Sweden.

The TEACCH method is built upon the core principles of structured teaching, including organizing the physical environment, providing a predictable sequence of activities, utilizing visual schedules, establishing routines and flexibility, implementing work/activity systems, and offering visually structured activities.

Beyond its specific focus on autism, the TEACCH method utilizes visual cues to make learning more accessible, particularly for non-verbal children. Visual aids turn to learn into a universal tool, capitalizing on children's strengths to help them grasp the "where-how-when-how long" of events, fostering their independence in managing their own time.

The primary goal of the TEACCH method is to equip children on the autism spectrum with social skills and positively transform their perception of social environments. Clarifying pedagogy influences adaptive behaviors, social reciprocity, parental stress levels, and parent-child interactions.

Another advantage of the TEACCH method is that when parents are educated and can apply this teaching approach at home, the child's behavior becomes more adaptable within their everyday routines, thereby reducing parental stress. Parents' involvement in implementing this method not only enhances its effectiveness but also contributes to the child's independence and improved social integration.

As a social pedagogue, I consider my role in supporting and assisting children in the school setting, as well as providing everyday support and education to parents, crucial. The low-arousal approach emphasizes strategies focused on reducing stress, fear, and frustration. These strategies aim to prevent dysregulation and avoid crisis situations. By understanding the situation, identifying triggers, and using low-intensity solutions, we can proactively apply this approach to learning and educational environments. I eagerly anticipate working with this method, as it promotes a relaxed and calm atmosphere, where nobody argues when they feel at ease.

From my social pedagogue perspective, adopting a low-arousal approach to teaching entails maintaining a calm, consistent learning environment. This begins with getting to know the students, establishing fixed routines and structure, and approaching the work with a positive attitude.

If we wish to effect change, we must take responsibility. It can never be solely the individual's fault, just as it can never be anyone else's fault if you have a problem. It is my responsibility if I have a problem, and no one else's.

Admittedly, it may seem harsh from this perspective: there are no unmotivated children with neurodevelopmental disorders; there are only educators and parents who are less skilled at motivation. By internalizing this principle in our daily lives, we can enhance the lives of both children and their families.

As educators or parents, we often believe that we need to control children with special needs. Only when a child possesses full self-control and autonomy they can meet expectations. Therefore, every school and family must work to enhance a child's self-control.

Navigating Through Harassment and Discrimination in Schools

I'd like to bring you along on my journey as a social pedagogue — a path that often leads to confronting some harsh realities. In our schools, beneath the surface of daily routines and the humdrum of learning, there exists a darker side — the prevalence of discrimination, harassment, and derogatory treatment.

Recently, I read an intriguing report by the Swedish National Agency for Education titled, "Discriminated, Harassed, Offended? Children's, students' and adult learners' Perceptions of Discrimination and Harassment". The findings of this report, based on interviews with over 500 children, students, and adult learners, are eye-opening and crucial for anyone working within the realm of social pedagogy.

Discrimination, harassment, and derogatory treatment occur daily in every school, affecting both students and staff. The most striking revelation was that boys are often the most victimized and simultaneously the prime perpetrators of verbal and physical threats.

These occurrences are commonly tied to homophobia, racism, or appearance-based bullying. Girls, on the other hand, tend to rely more on spreading rumors and backbiting, with the bulk of their negative interactions revolving around body shaming. They are also frequently subjected to sexual harassment, primarily in elementary schools.

This persistent behavior threatens the sense of security within our schools. Faced with such behavior, it's clear that tackling discrimination requires a differentiated approach for boys and girls. For girls, creating safe spaces within schools is critical. For boys, fostering a supportive environment through dedicated teams seems most effective.

The Swedish Education Act establishes that school operations must align with fundamental democratic values. Every individual within the school environment must promote respect for human dignity and our shared environment. Special emphasis is placed on promoting gender equality and actively countering all forms of offensive behavior, such as bullying and racist behaviors.

However, despite the clear guidelines, most students are unaware of the existing protection laws and equal treatment plans, as noted by the Swedish National Agency for Education. This lack of knowledge fosters an environment where norms related to discrimination, harassment, and offensive behavior go unchallenged.

In my role as a social pedagogue, I see it as my responsibility to foster open relations with students, to be the adult they feel safe with. Regular conversations with parents, participation in school activities, increased vigilance, and constant upholding of core values are tools I intend to use.

The question that I now pose to you, dear readers, is this — what are your thoughts on the fact that all discrimination, harassment, and derogatory treatment are tied to norms? How can we better educate our children about these norms to foster a safer and more inclusive learning environment?

These are challenging issues to address, but the first step is always to initiate the conversation. I believe that together, we can pave the way for a future where every child feels safe, included, and respected in our schools.

Adapting Learning Environments for Children With ADHD

In my journey as a social pedagogue, one key insight has stood out: the secret to motivating a child with ADHD lies not in altering the child, but in adapting and modifying the learning environment. So often, educators devote considerable time and effort in an attempt to change the child. However, their time might be more efficiently used in rethinking the routines and procedures they implement with the child.

As a social pedagogue, I am a professional who works with children to help with personal growth, development, and well-being. The role can encompass aspects of education, psychology, and social work. I aim to help children develop their potential, live fulfilling lives, and contribute meaningfully to their communities, often through educational and socially supportive measures.

As much as possible, the curriculum should be engaging and relevant, catering to the child's unique characteristics and potential. This resonates with what I've read in "Autism and ADHD in High School

Part 2: Clarifying Pedagogy" by David Edfelt, Annelie Karlsson, Ann Lindgren, and Anna Sjölund. Implementing a curriculum that is irrelevant to students' interests generally leads to disruptive behavior, poor academic performance, limited progress, and in some cases dropouts.

Children with ADHD live very much in the present. Long-term goals and rewards (grades or merit values) are often ineffective motivators for them.

In my professional reflection, I've pondered over how I, as a social pedagogue, can assist in a classroom setting that accommodates children with different diagnoses. I've come across various teaching strategies that can bolster motivation, as detailed in both the books and various articles I've read. Some of these strategies include:

1. Providing a structured, predictable environment.
2. Offering simple, one-step instructions.
3. Using simultaneous verbal and visual inputs, like dictating instructions while writing them on the board.
4. Clearly stating rules, boundaries, and expectations and prominently displaying them.
5. Allowing occasional breaks for the child to relax and rejuvenate.
6. Acknowledging the child's need for movement and activity by designing classroom activities that encourage movement.
7. Gaining the child's attention before providing guidance or instructions. This can be achieved by saying his name or using a hand signal.
8. Focusing on quality over quantity. Long, complex tasks are challenging for a child with attention difficulties.
9. Allowing the child ample time (10 to 15 seconds) to respond to verbal questions. Processing and understanding the

question can take some time. When possible, supplement verbal questions with visual input.

10. Refraining from attributing judgmental reasons for the child's inconsistency and impulsivity. Remember, these behaviors occur without the child's fault or choice.

11. Recognizing that hyperactive behaviors during seated work (like drumming fingers or tapping a pen) are a release for the child's hyperactivity. Unless these movements are distracting or disruptive to others, ignore them.

12. Giving the child with ADHD opportunities to showcase divergent, creative, and imaginative thinking and to receive recognition for their originality.

13. Trying alternative assessment methods, such as oral testing or demonstration testing. Written tests and evaluations can be challenging for children with attention difficulties due to their linguistic and organizational weaknesses.

14. Never take good behavior for granted. Praise and reinforce the child for not interrupting, working patiently, staying in place, and cooperating.

Together, we can unlock the full potential of children with ADHD, giving them the opportunity to thrive in a setting that not only understands but also embraces their unique way of learning and interacting with the world. Let's journey toward this more inclusive and empathetic approach to education, one classroom at a time.

How Holistic Education Contributes to Children's Well-Being and Success

My role extends beyond the conventional understanding of an educator. It's not just about teaching; it's about nurturing the holistic development of children. My mission is to foster an environment that empowers students to reach their full potential, enabling them to become responsible, self-aware, and compassionate individuals.

Social pedagogy is a transdisciplinary approach that brings together theories and concepts from education, psychology, sociology, and philosophy. It aims to create learning environments that are nurturing, inclusive, and empowering, ensuring that each child's unique needs are met.

What makes social pedagogy unique is its emphasis on the relationship between the educator and the student. The relationship is not just about teaching and learning but is also about mutual respect, trust, and understanding. As a social pedagogue, I strive to build such relationships with my students.

However, navigating the path of social pedagogy is not always easy. It requires a continuous quest for knowledge, insights, and resources that can support this holistic approach to education. In this journey, I found an invaluable partner in Tipsbanken, an online platform offering a wealth of resources aimed at supporting children across all stages of education.

The resources on Tipsbanken have been transformative to my practice. For example, the seminars by psychologist David Edfelt provided actionable strategies for creating conducive learning environments and managing challenging behaviors in classrooms. By implementing these strategies, I observed improvements in classroom dynamics, reduced stress levels, and a more positive learning atmosphere.

Moreover, Tipsbanken also provides resources for parents, enhancing their ability to navigate complex educational scenarios. This aids in improving parent-teacher relationships, fostering a cooperative and constructive environment.

Through social pedagogy, we, as educators, can make significant strides in promoting children's overall well-being and academic success. By fostering a supportive and holistic learning environment, we equip our students with the tools they need to flourish in and outside the classroom.

As I continue my journey as a social pedagogue, I am excited about the positive change can bring to my students and the broader school community. I am eager to see the fruits of this approach, as each student progresses, growing into the best version of themselves.

Girls and ADHD: Historical Overview and Emergent Research

Supporting Girls with ADHD

I want to share with you a deeply personal and heartfelt perspective as a social pedagogue working with children, specifically focusing on the often overlooked group of girls with Attention-Deficit/Hyperactivity Disorder (ADHD). Throughout my career, I have witnessed the challenges and triumphs of countless children, but it is the silent struggles of these girls that have left an indelible mark on my heart.

The discrepancy in ADHD diagnosis and treatment between boys and girls is well-documented in research. Studies such as "Sex Differences in ADHD Symptom Severity" by Gaub and Carlson (1997)[1] highlight that while boys with ADHD often exhibit more externalizing behaviors, girls tend to internalize their symptoms. This divergence, coupled with societal expectations, often leads to girls with ADHD being underdiagnosed and misunderstood.

As a social pedagogue, my role transcends the traditional confines of education. Understanding and responding to the individual needs of each child forms the cornerstone of my practice. For girls with ADHD, who often present less noticeable symptoms such as inattention and disorganization, this individualized approach is not just beneficial — it's critical.

Adopting the framework established by theorists like Erik Erikson and Lev Vygotsky, I prioritize fostering a healthy socio-emotional environment, a key tenet of social pedagogy. This is of paramount importance in supporting girls with ADHD who, as observed by Rucklidge (2010)^[2^], often suffer from low self-esteem and internalized distress.

I strive to create a space of understanding and acceptance, encouraging girls to explore their interests and strengths. This empowerment-focused approach promotes their self-worth, fostering resilience, a critical attribute for girls with ADHD as outlined by Owens & Hinshaw (2013)^[3^].

Through close collaboration with parents, teachers, and therapists, I aim to foster a consistent and supportive environment for these young individuals. This community-oriented approach, drawn from the principles of social pedagogy, helps them to better manage their ADHD symptoms and harness their unique potential.

In the field of ADHD, the prevailing image has been that of hyperactive boys. However, research and my own experiences have shown that girls with ADHD are often misunderstood and overlooked. The diagnostic criteria and assessment tools, primarily developed based on research with boys, fail to adequately capture the unique presentation of ADHD in girls (Arnold, L.E., 1996). This gender bias has led to underdiagnosis and delayed interventions for many girls, leaving them without the understanding, support, and treatment they desperately need.

Studies have shown that the prevalence of ADHD in girls may be more comparable to boys than previously thought (Kopp et al., 2005; Ramtekkar et al., 2010). However, societal expectations and misconceptions have perpetuated the belief that ADHD primarily affects boys, causing girls' symptoms to be dismissed or misattributed. Allow me to share with you the story of Anna, a bright and articulate girl whom I had the privilege of working with. Anna's teachers saw her as a daydreamer rather than recognizing her potential ADHD symptoms. Sadly, Anna's story is all too common, and it is these girls' struggles that have inspired me to advocate for more inclusive ADHD diagnoses.

One significant turning point in my career was a five-year study conducted in Gothenburg. We embarked on a mission to educate staff members about ADHD, distributed ADHD questionnaires to parents, and involved doctors in conducting neuropsychiatric assessments. The results were eye-opening: we identified ten times more girls with ADHD by the end of the study (Kopp & Gillberg, 2003). This finding was both heartening and a stark reminder of how many girls might have fallen through the cracks over the years.

A crucial lesson I learned is the role of age in ADHD diagnosis. Boys are often diagnosed between the ages of 6 and 12, while girls, like Anna, often receive their diagnosis after the age of 12 (Kopp & Gillberg, 2003). It seems that our bright, daydreaming girls may exhibit different symptoms than their male peers, leading to delayed diagnosis and intervention. This delayed recognition can have long-lasting effects, hindering their academic, social, and emotional development.

Moreover, it is essential to recognize that ADHD does not solely affect children. In recent years, there has been an increase in adults seeking help for ADHD symptoms, and surprisingly, more women than men have been identified (Nylander et al., 2009). This revelation validates the silent struggles experienced by many women who have lived their lives without understanding why they felt different.

It is high time we move beyond stereotypes and embrace a more comprehensive understanding of ADHD. We must acknowledge that ADHD does not discriminate by gender and that girls with ADHD often manifest their symptoms differently. By doing so, we can create a more inclusive and supportive environment for these girls, empowering them to reach their full potential.

To achieve this, we need to address the inherent biases in our diagnostic tools and criteria. We must develop gender-specific assessments that capture the nuanced presentation of ADHD in girls (Ohan, J.L., & Johnston, C., 2005). Teachers and healthcare professionals should be aware of the distinctive behaviors exhibited by girls with ADHD and be open to considering ADHD as a possible explanation for their struggles. By enhancing awareness and providing tailored support, we can ensure that girls with ADHD receive the recognition, understanding, and assistance they deserve.

Our goal should not merely be to 'treat' or 'manage' ADHD. Instead, we should strive to empower girls with ADHD, helping them understand that they can channel their unique strengths and perspectives into meaningful contributions.

I invite you to join me in broadening the narrative around ADHD, particularly in girls. Together, we can enhance awareness, foster understanding, and ensure that our support systems truly cater to the needs of all individuals with ADHD.

As we continue on this journey, let's remember that in the words of Fred Rogers, "Anyone who does anything to help a child in his life is a hero to me."

Freedom in the Classroom

Free Zones in Education

The struggle against honor-related violence and oppression isn't confined to law enforcement or social work. It's an integral aspect of our educational system — a battleground where we can shape minds, build resilience, and empower victims to break free from oppressive societal norms. As a social pedagogue, I strive daily to transform the classrooms I engage with into 'free zones', safe spaces where students can freely express their identities and reach their potential, far away from the confines of honor-related norms.

A social pedagogue's role merges education, social work, and community development to nurture the holistic development of the individual. We work in close partnerships with teachers, parents, and students themselves to create an environment that promotes emotional, social, and academic growth.

In the fight against oppression, education holds the power to transform lives, kindle curiosity, and liberate the oppressed. Honor-related violence, known as hedersvåld in Sweden, leaves a debilitating imprint on the lives of its predominantly female victims. This reality is confronted daily by social pedagogues, especially those working with organizations such as FreeZone Sweden, who strive to create a safe and liberating environment for young people and to combat honor-related violence. This approach actively integrates tools and techniques into everyday work to create a safer and more inclusive learning environment.

FreeZone Sweden was established in 2013 by social worker and award-winning entrepreneur Johanna Salama. Salama's experiences working to empower young girls exposed her to the limitations imposed on their lives due to honor-related norms. The Free Zone method was originally developed in Germany, with the aim to provide a space free from prejudice and discrimination. The method was adopted and established in Sweden under the umbrella of the TRIS1[1] organization (Tjejers Rätt I Samhället (Girls' Rights in Society or TRIS). FreeZone Sweden aims to create an equal and secure society where every child and youth can grow up to understand their worth, build their identities, and live freely.

In the classroom, the struggle against honor-related violence takes on significant importance. The FreeZone methodology, Fria Zoner, is actively integrated into the everyday work of social pedagogues and certified Zoneledares. Zoneledare training provides the necessary knowledge and tools to combat honor-related violence, promoting an increased sense of coherence (KASAM) and building on solution-focused conversational methodology.

KASAM, or Känsla Av SAMmanhang, refers to a person's ability to perceive life as comprehensible, manageable, and meaningful. This concept plays a pivotal role in building resilience and empowering victims of honor-related violence. It is a Swedish term introduced by Aaron Antonovsky in his salutogenic model of health. It is often translated as the "Sense of Coherence" (SOC) in English. Antonovsky suggests that the stronger one's sense of coherence, the better one is at handling stress and maintaining good health.

In the context of honor-related violence and oppression, developing a strong KASAM is crucial. It supports the victims' understanding of their circumstances, provides them with coping mechanisms, and ultimately, helps them find meaning in their struggles. In this way, KASAM becomes an essential tool for resilience and empowerment.

---

1. https://chat.openai.com/?model=gpt-4#user-content-fn-1_0bcef9c45bd8a48eda1b26eb0c61c8

Fria Zoner serves as a beacon of freedom for students aged 11–25 living under honor-related norms. It serves as a 'free zone' where students can escape the confines of oppressive societal norms and begin to create their own identities. The method raises the KASAM, building on solution-focused conversational methodology, active value exercises, relaxation, and forum games.

My role as a social pedagogue isn't just about promoting academic achievement. It goes much deeper than that — it's about fostering a community where each student can live free from the constraints of oppressive norms, express their unique identities, and reach their full potential. Every day, I am privileged to see the transformative power of education as I work hand in hand with my students, using the tools and techniques of FreeZone to help them construct their identities and take control of their lives.

In Sweden, we are making great strides toward eradicating honor-related violence. But there's a lot more to be done, and education is at the heart of that effort. So let's work together — educators, parents, community leaders, and policymakers — to continue creating free zones where our young people can flourish. The struggle is tough, but with determination and the right tools, we can help every young person live a life free from oppression.

John Dewey's Philosophy Towards Enlightened Action

One of my most enlightening journeys has been delving into the world of John Dewey, a renowned American philosopher, and educator whose ideas continue to resonate powerfully in my practice. My deep-seated interest in Dewey's philosophies started during my formative years in the field when I had the opportunity to study some of his most influential texts.

Dewey, who spanned the 19th and 20th centuries, has been recognized as one of the classics in pedagogy. Not only was he an acclaimed teacher and philosopher, but he also advocated fiercely for the teacher's profession. He argued that teaching was an honorable occupation that required high-level education, talent, and respect. Dewey's ideas were revolutionary and still hold substantial weight in our contemporary society.

My connection to Dewey's work was established in a Swedish anthology published about twenty years ago that encompassed several of his shorter texts (Individ, School and Society, 1980). Dewey's writings served as a reference point for modern pedagogical ideas and school politics rhetoric. This ignited a spark within me and compelled me to delve deeper into his insightful perspectives.

Understanding Dewey's holistic view of human action has been paramount in shaping my pedagogical approach. He argued that our actions — be they esthetic, political, ethical, or other forms of actions — are intrinsically intertwined and cannot be separated from each other or from the social contexts in which they are performed. As a social pedagogue, I found this idea to be particularly profound, and it has since become a guiding principle in my work.

Incorporating Dewey's holistic perspective into my social pedagogy practice has encouraged me to continuously reassess my multifaceted perceptions and actions, not only in education but in my personal interactions as well. My experiences in the field are no longer merely about delivering knowledge or facilitating activities; they are opportunities for enlightenment, reflection, and transformation.

By embracing Dewey's teachings, I aim to foster a democratic lifestyle that underlines the importance of communication, sympathy, and mutual respect. In every interaction I engage in, I strive to incorporate these principles in a meaningful way. This approach has proven to be a powerful tool in addressing various social challenges and improving the quality of life of those I work with.

In conclusion, John Dewey's philosophy continues to serve as a lighthouse in my professional journey. It has not only enhanced my understanding of social pedagogy but also enriched my personal life. As a committed social pedagogue, I encourage fellow professionals and learners to dive into Dewey's work. His timeless wisdom is a beacon of light that will undoubtedly illuminate your path in this rewarding field.

Teaching Children with Challenging Behaviors

I've had the privilege of encountering the intricate world of childhood development from both professional and personal lenses. This unique perspective has shaped my understanding, particularly regarding children with challenging behaviors, such as those with diagnoses like NDD.

There is an increasing interest in children's mental health and those with psychological conditions. We, as parents, educators, and caregivers, face the challenge of creating a profound understanding through empathy and compassion for what the child experiences internally.

Embracing Empathy

A study by Peck et al. (2014) explored how teachers expressed genuine empathy toward students in their early school years. It revealed that true empathy involves using one's inner capabilities, such as thought and emotion, to sense the situation and feel for the other. Crucially, this should be done out of the free will, not coercion.

Empathy not only helps teachers to understand, feel, communicate, and respond to the student's needs but also the family's needs. Waite (2011) emphasizes active listening and having a good understanding through perspective-taking. Relationships, being vulnerable, should be handled with humble care.

Building Ethical Learning Environments

According to Bergmark (2009), the establishment of an ethical learning environment significantly impacts students' learning processes. Respectful interaction between teachers and students, where appreciation, engagement, respect, and participation, become key elements in the school's activities. This environment fosters motivation, encouragement, and affirmation.

Studies such as Greenes (1997) reveal specific insights, like boys with ADHD are more prone to develop addiction problems. Here the school's responsibility to prevent these issues becomes paramount. A positive approach to students' strengths to find solutions instead of focusing on problems is crucial.

The Importance of Reflective Practices

We must be conscious of our influence on children's motivation through our responses (Bergmark, 2009). This involves a conscious empathetic approach and putting compassion before pity.

Challenges in daily interaction may stem from an overemphasis on either cognitive or affective abilities (Kinge, 2015). Research by O'Kearney et al. (2016) indicated that children with ODD (Oppositional Defiant Disorder) have a reduced ability to describe causes for feelings, and handle and respond to them well.

The Crossroads of Culture and Democracy

In the context of multicultural Sweden, Zackari and Modigh's "The Value Foundation Book — About Conversations for Democracy in School"(2000), highlights the increasing interest in core values and democracy. The classroom becomes a meeting place for different values, cultures, religions, and social environments. Conveying society's fundamental values is not an easy task but is encompassing and essential.

Final Thoughts

As a social pedagogue and a parent, I can affirm that the journey toward understanding, empathy, and compassion is continuous and complex. The professional and personal interplay guides us to a better realization of the children's world. Together, we can make strides in nurturing, supporting, and inspiring these young minds to flourish.

Building Connections: Pedagogues' Empathy and Students' Success

Empathy has increasingly become a subject of interest, extending into various fields of human interactions. In the realm of education, particularly among teachers and students, it offers a compelling area of exploration. Empathy relies on factors rooted in self-awareness and the ability to empathize, leading to enhanced abilities to read non-verbal cues such as gestures, tones, and facial expressions. As a social pedagogue with a specialization in working with children with Neurodevelopmental Disorders (NDD), and as a mother of three wonderful sons, I have seen firsthand how an empathetic approach can be a success factor in a student's education.

Understanding Empathy

The term "empathy" has its origin in the German word "einfühlung," meaning the ability to adopt an objective position and be understanding of another person's experience. Empathy involves recognizing others' feelings and responding to them with compassion and understanding. While empathy emphasizes understanding, sympathy deals with sharing the experience (Ruusuvuori, 2005; Bohlin & Eklund, 2013).

Empathy in the Classroom

In every classroom, there are students with varying needs. Teachers are expected to respond to these needs efficiently and in an individually tailored way, as clearly stated under norms and values in the Swedish primary school curriculum (Lgr 11, 2011). Empathetic handling by the teacher proves to be a success factor for the student in their schooling (Kutscher, 2010). In my work with children diagnosed with NDD, patience, understanding, and creativity have been essential. Each child is a unique puzzle, and unraveling that puzzle is a journey filled with meaningful interactions and breakthroughs.

The Impact of Empathetic Treatment

Empathetic treatment is about seeing others and providing the right affirmation at the right time. Research shows that children's success in social interaction depends on the adult's empathetic handling (Kinge, 2015; Rogers, 1975). Being a mother has taught me resilience, compassion, and the value of unconditional support. I've been able to leverage these qualities in my professional practice, forging strong connections with children and their families.

Empathy, Sympathy, and Complexity

The relationship between empathy and sympathy is complex. Some psychologists warn against confusing these concepts, while others describe how they intertwine (Bohlin & Eklund, 2013; Strandberg, 2015). Several studies highlight the empathetic effect of facial expressions (Izard, 1990; Sonnby-Borgström, 2003). My philosophy of pedagogy emphasizes collaboration, communication, and emotional intelligence. A holistic approach where mental, emotional, and social aspects are considered in tandem creates a nurturing environment.

Final Thoughts

Empathy is a vital element in the relationship between teachers and students. Teachers' empathy serves as a powerful source for students' development, promoting cooperation, trust, and mutual growth (Balldin & Hedevåg, 2013). Implementing empathy as a key principle in educational settings may pave the way for a more humane and successful approach to learning.

In the end, my work as a social pedagogue and a mother has been about building relationships and creating a space where growth occurs naturally and joyfully. The intricate dance of pedagogy and parenting has shaped me, and I'm grateful every day for the opportunity to make a positive impact. My heart and soul are dedicated to this cause, and I will continue to embrace it with all the passion, wisdom, and love that I have.

Understanding Ourselves: Exploring the Depths of the Mind Through Sigmund Freud's Psychoanalytic Perspective

I've come to deeply value diverse perspectives that provide insights into the rich tapestry that makes up the human mind. Among the multitude of views, one that has significantly influenced the way I see people and their behaviors is the psychodynamic view, a perspective initially championed by the groundbreaking Sigmund Freud (1856–1939). Freud's theories, while occasionally met with skepticism and critique, have undeniably revolutionized our understanding of human psychology.

My norm-critical stance aligns well with Freud's defiance of societal norms and taboos, as he fearlessly broached subjects such as sexuality and mental health treatments that were previously suppressed. His work has unquestionably influenced the psychology field, despite some claiming his theories lack a rigorous scientific foundation.

Moreover, Freud's emphasis on childhood experiences and their significant impact on adult lives has resonated with me not only professionally, but also personally. As a mother to three boys, I prioritize shaping their childhood in a way that prepares them to be empathetic and inclusive adults who embrace diverse perspectives. Freud's concept of the lasting impression our early years have on our adulthood is an idea we will delve into further in this article.

The Dynamics of Personality: Id, Ego, Superego

Freud's dynamic model underscores the unconscious aspects of personality. According to Freud, the personality comprises three levels of consciousness — the conscious, the preconscious, and the unconscious — and three subsystems known as the id, the ego, and the superego.

The id, being the most primitive aspect of our personality, represents our basic biological drives such as sex and aggression. These drives demand immediate gratification without considering rationality or reason. The ego is the mediator, juggling between the demands of the id and the rules imposed by the superego while keeping in touch with reality. The superego, on the other hand, acts as our moral compass, instilled by societal norms and expectations, rewarding us when we conform and inducing feelings of guilt when we stray. This constant interaction among these three subsystems, influenced by our early experiences, shapes our personality and behavior.

Exploring the Mind's Layers: The Topographical Model

In Freud's topographical model, the mind is divided into three layers: the conscious, the preconscious, and the unconscious. The conscious layer contains feelings, thoughts, and experiences we are presently aware of. The preconscious layer holds information that can be recalled and brought into consciousness when needed. The unconscious layer, however, is a repository of memories, thoughts, and feelings inaccessible to our conscious mind. It often contains painful or traumatic experiences from our childhood, which our mind suppresses to protect us.

Unveiling Our Defence Mechanisms

To cope with life's challenges and internal conflicts, our ego employs various defense mechanisms. These mechanisms shield us from feelings of anxiety by altering our perception of reality, often unconsciously. It's important to note that while these defense mechanisms serve a protective function, overreliance on them can lead to problems as it requires considerable psychic energy to keep them active.

Freud detailed several defense mechanisms including denial, rationalization, reaction formation, sublimation, regression, compensation, humor, identification, displacement, self-punishment, projection, and repression. Each mechanism serves to guard us against distressing thoughts or feelings, but when overly used or relied upon, can interfere with our well-being and growth.

Childhood Development Stages

As both a Social Pedagogue and a mother, the importance of childhood experiences in shaping an individual's personality has been a cornerstone of my professional and personal journey. Freud's theories, which heavily underline this principle, suggest that unresolved conflicts or traumatic events from our formative years can surface as psychological problems in our adult lives. It's an idea that I've found profoundly impactful, reinforcing my belief that childhood indeed lays the bedrock for our personality, thereby making it an incredibly influential period in our personal evolution.

My work, focused on creating a tolerant, inclusive educational environment and teaching my three boys to grow into empathetic, broad-minded men, often brings Freud's theories into perspective. Understanding his psychoanalytic view does not merely enrich our comprehension of our behaviors, motivations, and emotional struggles, but also imparts crucial lessons for my approach as an educator and a parent.

Though Freud's theories have faced their fair share of criticism and are limited in certain aspects, they nonetheless present a comprehensive framework that urges us to delve deeper than the obvious, to explore the hidden recesses of our unconscious mind. These theories guide my ongoing quest for a deeper understanding of the human psyche, a quest I invite you to join me.

Fostering Hope and Success

My daily life revolves around nurturing relationships and empowering the individuals I work with. In this context, I've also had the privilege of working with children diagnosed with NDD (Neurodevelopmental Disorders). But more importantly, my journey has taught me that motivation is not a solitary concept confined to a classroom. It's a shared endeavor, a connection that brings together teachers, parents, students, and all those involved in the educational and social sphere.

Understanding Motivation: A Journey Beyond the Classroom

Motivation, as a central concept in pedagogical work, has a particular weight in teaching students who are facing challenges and within therapeutic contexts. People's explanations for successes and failures and the significance of expectations are especially focused. But it is essential to recognize that motivation isn't solely an individual trait; it's a result of one's experiences and the way one is treated.

The Importance of Bemötande (Approach)

The word "bemötande" in Swedish can translate to approach or response, and it's an essential aspect of motivation. It emphasizes the importance of how you are seen, not just that you are seen. It's about nurturing a positive relationship without reinforcing a dependent position. Good bemötande is the foundation for motivational work.

Pedagogy: More Than Just Teaching

Pedagogy often associates with education and upbringing. But it has a broader meaning. Essentially, pedagogy is about people's learning, social, and cultural integration processes, about participation in one's life and surrounding life. This core of pedagogy has been described as a multifaceted web of relationships created through pedagogical actions, with communication being one of its central aspects.

The Pygmalion Effect: Believing to Achieve

Pedagogical research has widely studied the Pygmalion effect, referring to how expectations can act as self-fulfilling prophecies. Positive expectations lead to good results, while negative expectations lead to adverse outcomes. This emphasizes the importance of maintaining a positive outlook on the students, encouraging them to strive, and believing in their ability to succeed.

The Role of a Pedagogue: Being Open and Reflective

Motivational work requires the pedagogue to have a positive view of their students and an open, listening attitude. This calls for critical reflection on one's work, openness to learning, and a conducive work environment. These aspects are vital in shaping the pedagogical encounter, where motivation and motivational work must be seen.

It's a Shared Journey

Motivation in the educational context is not just about igniting a spark in the student; it's about keeping the flame alive. It's a dynamic, ongoing process that involves not only the teacher and the student but everyone surrounding them. It's about empathy, understanding, and a genuine connection that fosters growth. As a social pedagogue and a mother, I witness this connection every day, and it's a dance, a continuous interplay of roles that shapes not just an educational journey but a life journey.

Understanding Gender-Specific Manifestations of ADHD

I am deeply committed to inclusive and supportive learning environments for children. In my role, I have had the privilege of working closely with girls who have ADHD, witnessing their unique challenges and triumphs. Drawing on my personal experiences and extensive research, this article aims to shed light on the specific manifestations of ADHD in girls and provide practical strategies to support their educational journey and home environments.

Recognizing Gender Disparities in ADHD:

ADHD, traditionally associated with hyperactivity and impulsivity, presents itself differently in girls compared to boys. While boys may exhibit more externalized symptoms, such as restlessness and disruptive behavior, girls often display internalized symptoms, including inattention, disorganization, and emotional dysregulation. Unfortunately, these internalized symptoms are frequently overlooked, leading to underdiagnosis or misdiagnosis in girls (Staller & Faraone, 2006).

Unveiling Genetic and Neurobiological Influences:

Early studies suggested a higher heritability rate of ADHD in boys, leading to the assumption that boys were more predisposed to the condition. However, more recent research has challenged this notion, indicating similar heritability rates across genders (Faraone et al., 2000; Rietveld et al., 2003). Furthermore, neurobiological investigations have highlighted the involvement of various brain regions, such as the prefrontal cortex, basal ganglia, and cerebellum, in ADHD. Imbalances in the dopaminergic and noradrenergic systems have also been implicated in the disorder's etiology (Stefanatos & Baron, 2007; Solanto, 2002).

A Deeper Understanding of Neurological Disparities:

Advanced imaging techniques, including MRI and fMRI, have provided valuable insights into the neurodevelopmental differences observed in ADHD. Studies have revealed structural and functional disparities in brain regions associated with attention processes. Notably, researchers have identified subtle variations between genders, underscoring the importance of considering gender-specific factors in understanding the neural underpinnings of ADHD (Valera et al., 2007; Hutchinson et al., 2008; Castellanos et al., 2001).

Challenges in Diagnosis and Intervention:

Diagnosing ADHD in girls poses particular challenges due to diagnostic criteria that were initially based on observations of boys. This discrepancy can lead to difficulties in recognizing ADHD in girls, whose symptoms may not align with the stereotypical presentation. Adopting gender-sensitive assessment tools and approaches is crucial to ensure accurate identification, enabling appropriate interventions and support (Nadeau & Quinn, 2002). Girls with ADHD face a unique set of challenges that can often go unnoticed or misunderstood. Due to their internalized symptoms, such as inattention and emotional dysregulation, they may fly under the radar, overshadowed by their more hyperactive male counterparts. Consequently, girls with ADHD are at risk of being overlooked for diagnostic assessment and may not receive the support they need to thrive academically and emotionally.

Addressing Societal Context:

In addition to biological and neurological factors, societal expectations and gender biases significantly influence the experiences of girls with ADHD. Cultural norms and stereotypes often contribute to the underestimation or dismissal of girls' struggles, resulting in delayed intervention and support. Recognizing and addressing these social factors are essential steps toward creating a more inclusive and equitable environment for girls with ADHD.

Understanding the Classroom Dynamics:

In the classroom, girls with ADHD may struggle with maintaining focus during lessons, organizing their assignments, and completing tasks independently. They might also find it challenging to manage their time effectively, leading to difficulties in meeting deadlines. Additionally, they may experience heightened sensitivity to criticism or social rejection, which can impact their self-esteem and overall well-being. Recognizing these challenges is crucial for educators and parents in providing targeted support and interventions.

Empowering Girls with ADHD:

Equipped with a deeper understanding of gender-specific manifestations, it is our collective responsibility to empower girls with ADHD. By fostering understanding, providing tailored interventions, and creating supportive environments, we can help these girls thrive. Collaboration among parents, educators, and healthcare professionals is vital in identifying strengths, addressing challenges, and promoting self-esteem and resilience.

Exploring the gender-specific dimensions of ADHD allows us to better understand and appreciate the unique experiences and challenges faced by girls. As a Social Pedagogue, my goal is to advocate for evidence-based practices that uplift and empower girls with ADHD, ensuring they receive the support they need within educational settings. By spreading awareness and fostering a compassionate and inclusive approach, we can help girls with ADHD reach their full potential.

Unveiling The Impact of Ellen Key on Modern Social Pedagogy

As I am deeply invested in the well-being and growth of children, I often find myself reflecting on the philosophical foundations that guide my practice. One influential figure who has profoundly shaped my professional journey is the pioneering Swedish pedagogue and writer, Ellen Key. Not only have her ideas formed the backbone of my academic studies, but they have also significantly influenced how I approach my day-to-day work with children and their families.

The Beginning

In the early 20th century, Ellen Key was a trailblazer in advocating for the rights of children and the transformation of educational systems. She stood out for her innovative and controversial theories about education and child upbringing, promoting a form of education that was grounded in the child's personality, rather than in rigid discipline and rote learning.

However, Key's stance on gender roles, and her belief in essential gender differences, could be seen as controversial today. She asserted that men and women are equal but fundamentally different, and she believed their education should reflect these differences. For instance, she suggested that women's education should not be overly intellectual, as she believed women were more receptive to impressions than opinions. Moreover, she saw women's educational paths as distinct from men's, an idea that has been criticized by some contemporary feminists.

The Approach

Key's pedagogical approach emphasized love, respect, and clear norms, aiming to foster both individuality and social responsibility within the child. Her critical view on rote learning and fragmented school days reflects the ongoing debate about effective learning methods. She promoted an education system in which children's own observations formed the basis for knowledge acquisition and where practical application, rather than memorization, was prioritized.

Her book, "The Century of the Child", despite its publication more than a century ago, continues to be influential, particularly in Germany where a new edition was released as recently as 1992. However, the book is hard to find in Sweden, with the last edition having been published in 1927.

The Theory

Despite the controversies and differing viewpoints, Ellen Key's lasting impact can be seen in her influence on the educational system and child rights, with many of her pedagogical principles reflected in Sweden's modern curriculum (Lpo 94). Her clear stance against corporal punishment was also a pioneering move that predated by nearly 80 years the 1979 Swedish law that forbade parents from physically disciplining their children.

While Ellen Key's theories may not be widely debated today, her work remains relevant in discussions around education and child rights. Her ideas, though embedded in her historical context, still have resonances today, particularly in relation to individualized learning and the recognition of children's rights. The nuanced understanding of her work is crucial to appreciate its contemporary relevance and potential future implications.

Applying Ellen Key´s Philosophy

My engagement with Key's philosophies started during my social pedagogy studies when I had the opportunity to delve into her groundbreaking book, "The Century of the Child." This early

20th-century text, which championed the idea of child-centered education long before it became the norm, resonated deeply with me. Key's unwavering belief in fostering individuality while respecting social responsibility, her emphasis on love, clear norms, and respect in pedagogical relationships, and her advocacy for practical application over rote memorization have become essential guiding principles in my practice.

In Key's vision for education, I found a validation of my instinctual beliefs about children's rights and the power of personalized learning. It offered a much-needed antidote to the more rigid, standardized models of education that often fail to nurture individuality. Her idea that education should emanate from the child's personality resonated with me, leading me to design learning experiences based on the unique needs, interests, and strengths of each child I work with.

Key's controversial views on gender roles and education, too, offer valuable insights. While her belief in distinct educational paths for boys and girls based on their inherent differences is debatable today, it raises important questions about how we consider gender in education. It's a reminder of the importance of ongoing dialogues about equality, diversity, and inclusion in pedagogical practices.

Applying Key's principles in my work, I have seen firsthand how a love-based, individualized approach to education can transform a child's learning journey. It brings out the best in children, encouraging them to grow into self-assured, empathetic, and socially responsible individuals. Key's influence has been instrumental in shaping my professional identity as a social pedagogue, prompting me to continually advocate for child-centered education that respects and nurtures each child's individuality.

A Personal Note

Reflecting on my professional journey, I cannot overstate the value of integrating theory and practice. The insights I gained from studying Key's work have profoundly shaped my understanding of social pedagogy and my role as a social pedagogue. I encourage my fellow professionals and anyone interested in education to delve into Key's work and other foundational texts. It is through this deep engagement with our intellectual heritage that we can continually evolve our practices, staying responsive to the ever-changing needs of children and society.

Ellen Key's philosophies may not be at the forefront of every pedagogical debate today, but her legacy persists in contemporary educational practices. Her ideas about child rights, individualized learning, and the importance of a love-based pedagogical approach are still relevant, offering valuable lessons for educators, social workers, and anyone dedicated to children's well-being.

As I continue my journey as a social pedagogue, I am grateful for the lessons I have learned from Ellen Key. They guide me every day in my mission to support the holistic development of each child I work with, reminding me that my work is not just about teaching, but also about nurturing, respecting, and empowering.

A Pedagogical Journey with Inclusive Behavior Support (IBIS)

Embracing change, reducing bullying, and building a positive learning environment for all

I know, I've said it all before, but I can't stress enough the importance of a safe and inclusive learning environment for all students. More importantly, as a single mother of three wonderful sons, I realize the impact that education and the school environment can have on young minds, even if two of my sons are now adults. Today, I want to share my thoughts on a concept that is transforming education in Sweden — Inclusive Behavior Support in Schools (IBIS).

What Is IBIS?

IBIS (Inkluderande beteendestöd i skolan) is an overarching model designed to foster an inclusive school through positive learning support. It aims to develop a positive school culture that strengthens students' academic achievements and social skills while preventing and managing problematic behaviors proactively.

Why IBIS Matters to Me: A Personal Insight

With a six-year-old son in school, I know the significance of having a robust framework to ensure that all levels of the school system are aligned with the values of inclusion and positivity. IBIS offers that framework. By reducing absenteeism, bullying, and anxiety, and enhancing classroom calmness and school performance, IBIS is a beacon of hope for many parents and educators like me.

Scientific Foundation of IBIS: Evidenced and Data-Driven

IBIS is rooted in models developed over the last 25 years. It builds on the fundamentals laid down by researchers at the University of Oregon and adapts other programs like SW-PBIS from the United States and PALS from Norway. It's evidence-based, relying on hundreds of research studies, and emphasizes data-driven decision-making. These robust foundations provide credibility and assurance that this model is built to succeed.

IBIS: Inclusive and Comprehensive

What makes IBIS unique is its inclusive nature. It involves the entire school — the principal, educators, and other staff members. It ensures a shared understanding of creating a positive and inclusive work environment, fulfilling the stipulations of the Swedish Education Act (2010).

Effects of IBIS: A Transformative Change

Studies have shown the wide-ranging positive effects of IBIS. From increased attendance to decreased behavioral problems, anxiety, and depression, and improved reading and mathematics skills, IBIS is more than a model; it's a revolutionary change. It's heartening to see how such a system can truly benefit my child, along with countless others.

Implementation and Training: Commitment to Excellence

Implementing IBIS takes careful planning and a shared commitment from the entire school, usually spanning 1–3 years. Training in IBIS is open to psychologists, special educators, counselors, or equivalent, and is offered in collaboration with Uppsala University.

A Parent's Perspective

As we continue to seek ways to nurture our children in a challenging world, IBIS is a beacon of hope. Its proven methods, comprehensive approach, and sincere commitment to inclusivity resonate with me as a professional and a mother.

This article is not just a technical explanation but a heartfelt insight into a system that can make our children's school experiences more enriching. May we all work together to create an educational environment where every child feels safe, valued, and encouraged to reach their fullest potential.

Inclusive Storytelling and The Power of Children's Literature

I want to talk about how children's literature, when handled with care and sensitivity, can be a transformative tool in shaping young minds.

And I'm going to do this by drawing from my personal experiences and insights as a social pedagogue and the rich knowledge you've shared.

As an individual devoted to educating and empowering children, I have an immense passion for stories. The role of representation in literature, especially children's literature, is one aspect of my job that I find most fascinating. So, let's dive into this thought-provoking subject and see where it takes us.

Reflecting societal norms: A look at "Harry Potter"

If you've ever read "Harry Potter and the Philosopher's Stone" by J.K. Rowling, you may remember how vividly the traditional gender roles were portrayed. Characters like Hermione Granger, an intelligent and caring young girl, and Ron Weasley, a brave and loyal young boy, embody typical feminine and masculine stereotypes. This emphasis on traditional gender roles can perpetuate societal norms about gender, sometimes in ways we don't fully realize.

Although books like "Harry Potter and the Philosopher's Stone" do not necessarily directly address cisgender, transgender, or queer experiences, they can serve as a tool to help children reflect on their identities and experiences. They can encourage children to express themselves, understand and empathize with others, and critically examine societal norms and expectations. For instance, simple questions such as, "How do you think it would feel to be Harry and not fit in?" or "What would it be like to change who you are like Professor McGonagall?" can lead to deeper discussions about identity and diversity.

The two sides of the coin: inclusivity and representation

It is, however, crucial to acknowledge the potential downside of this representation. For transgender and queer readers, the lack of representation of their experiences and identities can contribute to feelings of invisibility and exclusion. Meanwhile, cisgender readers may find the traditional gender roles and cisnormativity in the text affirming and validating, which can potentially lead to a more positive reading experience.

These differing experiences underscore the critical need for a broad spectrum of characters and narratives in children's literature. A range that captures not just diverse identities but also various experiences, helping children understand that there's no singular 'correct' way to be. Inclusivity should be the foundation of all literature.

Intersectionality: The confluence of multiple identities

This is where the concept of intersectionality comes into play. The term, coined by Kimberlé Williams Crenshaw, examines how different power structures and grounds for discrimination affect children and young people in school. For example, a student who identifies as both queer and non-white may face double marginalization due to their sexual orientation and race. By incorporating an intersectionality perspective within norm-critical pedagogy, teachers can equip students with the tools to question and critically examine societal norms and structures.

In this context, it becomes vital for teachers to evaluate the children's literature they present to their students, not only based on its literary value but also on the representations and norms it conveys. A useful resource here can be Lena Kåreland's book, "Skönlitteratur för barn och unga: historik, genrer, termer, analyser" ("Fiction for Children and Young People: History, Genres, Terms, Analyses") which delves into the historical development, genres, and analysis methods of children's literature.

We also need to be mindful of how we approach these discussions in learning environments. According to Läroplan (Lgr 22) för grundskolan samt för förskoleklassen och fritidshemmet ("Curriculum (Lgr 22) for Swedish Primary School, Pre-school Class, and Leisure-time Center") teaching should be based on a holistic view of the students and their needs, interests, and experiences.

By nurturing children's understanding of societal norms and expectations through literature, and by including a diversity of characters and experiences in children's literature, we can contribute to a more inclusive and understanding society. In our rapidly changing digital age, it's more important than ever for teachers to navigate and leverage these resources effectively. Hence, teacher education and training in this area should be prioritized.

In summary, the conversation on gender and gender identity is relevant in Swedish society as it promotes equality, informs policy and legislation, promotes education and awareness, and increases cultural exchange and representation. By continuously exploring and analyzing these issues, we can continue to work towards a more equitable and inclusive society in Sweden.

The Art of Formative Feedback

I understand the importance of nurturing growth and development in young minds. Being a single mother of three wonderful sons, I know firsthand the impact that effective guidance and feedback can have on a child's growth. It's the little steps that build the bridge to success. And in this educational journey, feedback in the classroom stands as a pivotal component. Let's delve into what research says about feedback strategies and how they shape our children's future.

The Purpose of Feedback

According to Shute (2008), formative feedback serves as information to guide students in altering their thinking and actions, with the ultimate goal of enhancing learning. Both Hattie and Timperley (2007) assert that feedback should propel the student from their current level of knowledge to their intended goal. The primary objective is to boost the student's knowledge, skills, and understanding in a particular subject area or skill such as problem-solving.

Types and Functions of Feedback

Feedback comes in various forms, such as specific response, goal-oriented, or immediate feedback while the student works on a task. Different functions of feedback are observed, ranging from direct and specific to facilitating feedback, provided in the form of suggestions to aid the student's learning.

1. Goal-Oriented Feedback: Shute (2008) emphasizes that this type of feedback offers information about progress toward a desired goal. To maintain motivation, the student needs to see that they can achieve it.

2. Immediate vs. Delayed Feedback: Practical subjects often involve immediate feedback, while theoretical subjects might experience a delay. In the practical environment, the connection between feedback and improvement is more explicit (William & Leahy, 2015).

3. The Classroom Context: Research by Havnes, Smith, Dysthe, and Ludvigsen (2012) highlights the contrasting feedback cultures in vocational training compared to theoretical subjects. The study revealed a prevalent lack of feedback culture, with more frequent feedback in practical vocational subjects.

4. Self-Assessment and Metacognitive Feedback: Encouraging students to understand and manage their learning can lead to them assessing their performance and finding strategies to move forward (Hattie & Timperley, 2007).

Challenges and Misconceptions

Feedback can be sporadic, and its practice may depend on the individual teacher's pedagogical stance (Havnes et al., 2012). Often, teachers might overestimate the quality of their feedback, and some students might overlook it, focusing solely on grades.

Towards a Brighter Future

As we nurture our children's minds, formative feedback at the task, process, and metacognitive levels can significantly contribute to their growth. Understanding each child's unique journey and providing relevant, specific, and timely feedback can foster a more engaging and fruitful learning experience.

A Personal Note

As a mother who has watched her children grow, I can testify that feedback is more than a classroom strategy; it's a life lesson. It's about learning to accept, adapt, and advance. Together, we can make education a journey of self-discovery, growth, and success. Together, let's make education not just a pursuit of knowledge but a pathway to wisdom.

A Comprehensive Approach to Anxiety and Panic Disorder for Modern Families

How anxiety management techniques can revolutionize our connection with ourselves and our loved ones

Living as a Social Pedagogue and a single mother, I can attest to the fact that anxiety, stress, and panic disorders are not foreign to many of us. The challenges of juggling family, career, and personal growth can be overwhelming, leading to detrimental effects on our overall well-being. This article illuminates a technique known as Applied Relaxation (AR) that has shown promise in managing anxiety and stress, not just in the clinical setting but in our homes as well.

Bridging Therapeutic Insights with Family Dynamics

Applied Relaxation Technique: AR, a method created to counter anxiety and panic disorders, resonates deeply with my personal journey as a mother and professional. The technique empowers us to recognize the early signs of anxiety and take control. It reminds me of teaching my youngest son to face his fears, helping him understand that he has the power to control his reactions.

Mechanisms of Action: As a single parent, the "vicious circle" model applied in AR often mirrors the repetitive cycle of stress and anxiety in our daily lives. Just as AR aims to break this cycle, I've learned that recognizing triggers and changing our response can also transform family dynamics.

Embracing Techniques: A Personal Success Story

Factors Contributing to AR's Success: Incorporating AR into my own life has not only reduced tension but enhanced my self-confidence as a mother. This success has translated into a more harmonious home, where understanding and communication thrive.

Prior Research and Applications: AR's flexibility is evident in its application across various ailments, from migraines to insomnia. This adaptability speaks to its potential within family environments, where diverse challenges abound.

Mindfulness: An Adjunctive Approach: I've witnessed the transformative power of mindfulness. Integrating mindfulness with AR has enriched my relationship with my children, fostering a more attentive and compassionate connection.

A Compassionate Path Forward

Applied Relaxation and Mindfulness aren't just theoretical concepts but practical tools that have enriched my life as a single mother and professional. They offer a compassionate pathway to understanding ourselves and those around us. By continuing to explore these techniques, we pave the way for more fulfilling relationships and a better quality of life.

A Guide to Psychoeducation & Positive Parenting

I feel a profound connection to the subject of psychoeducation. This personal connection has shaped my beliefs, my actions, and my dedication to supporting families through the challenges that come with childhood trauma.

Psychoeducation: A Fundamental Part of Healing

Psychoeducation forms the core of trauma-focused cognitive-behavioral therapy (TF-CBT). From the moment a child and their family come into contact with care, it must permeate the entire treatment process.

Normalizing Reactions

The purpose of psychoeducation is to normalize the child's and parent's reactions to the trauma and to strengthen helpful thoughts. This initial approach involves providing general information about the trauma, such as its occurrence, who it affects, its perpetrators, why it happens, and its effects. Such information needs to be age-appropriate and can be shared through written materials for further reading between sessions.

Addressing Misconceptions

Children and families affected by trauma often harbor incorrect thoughts and perceptions that may hinder the healing process. Correcting this information is crucial.

Providing Hope and Motivation

Psychoeducation also aims to convey hope and motivate treatment by informing about effective treatments, particularly TF-CBT, and instilling confidence that symptoms can improve.

Direct Symptom Management

Helping children and families cope with specific distressing symptoms, such as sleep problems, can foster hope and motivation for further treatment.

Learning Behaviors: Understanding the Basics

Children learn behaviors through multiple means,

- Consequences: Attention vs. Ignoring

Consequences play a significant role in shaping a child's actions. Praising a behavior often leads to an increase in that behavior. However, negative attention might inadvertently reinforce undesirable behaviors. Strategies to enhance positive behaviors and reduce negative ones include immediate praise and ignoring unwanted actions.

- Observation: Mimicry and Example

"Children don't do what you say; they do what you do"(Barn gör inte som du säger, de gör som du gör). Observation plays a vital role in children learning positive and negative behaviors. With the proper support, negative behaviors can be replaced with positive ones.

- Association: Linking Actions with Outcomes

Children also learn through association. For instance, associating pain with a hot stove leads to avoidance. Similarly, traumatic associations can be relearned in a safe environment.

PRAISE: The Power of Positive Attention

Praising a child's positive behavior is essential in reinforcing those actions. However, not all praise is created equal. Here are guidelines to ensure that your praise is effective and meaningful.

Guidelines for Effective Praise

1. Immediate: Praise the desired behavior as soon as it occurs.
2. Consistent and Predictable: Regularly reward positive behavior.
3. Specific: Clearly define what behavior you appreciate.
4. Entirely Positive: Avoid negative comments in your praise.
5. Enthusiastic and Joyful: Show genuine happiness in your praise.
6. Focus on Behaviors: Praise achievements and avoid superlatives.

A Heartfelt Note from a Mother

As a mother, I understand the vital role these guidelines play in nurturing a child's growth. Positive reinforcement has been an essential tool in my parenting journey, and I can't emphasize enough the power it holds.

Homework for Parents: Practice Specific Praise

- Identify a positive behavior you'd like to see more of.
- Follow the guidelines above to praise this behavior every time

it occurs.

- Don't wait for the full execution; praise every step or attempt.

Reflect on the specific behavior you chose to praise, describe an instance, and evaluate your feelings and the child's reaction.

In the world of both professional social pedagogy and personal parenting, understanding, acknowledging, and guiding are key. May this information bring enlightenment, encouragement, and empowerment to your family's journey. As someone who has walked this path, I share this with you, from one parent to another, with all my heart.

Navigating The Complex World of Pedagogy in The Information Age

I have not only seen the world through the eyes of an educator but also experienced it through the lens of a parent. This duality of roles has helped me understand the complexities of pedagogy and its interplay with human relationships.

Today, I want to share with you my reflections on pedagogy, a subject often misunderstood and yet deeply intertwined with our daily lives.

Pedagogy: A Mystical and Grounded Profession

Many people perceive pedagogues as engaged in a free and unbound stroll through life. They often see us educators as observers of the human journey, where everything is a game of subtle signals and complex negotiations. However, this view is only partially true.

Pedagogy is more than just a playful pursuit; it's an essential part of our knowledge and information society. It shapes our collective, goal-oriented, and conscious school development. With a broad perspective covering Swedish, Nordic, European, and Western educational philosophies, it is no mere child's play (Ljunghill 1999; Larsson 1993).

The Pedagogue: An Enigmatic Figure

Pedagogues might seem like ordinary people, but each one can be unique, mysterious, and inscrutable. What does a pedagogue see, and why should we care about human perspectives, relationships, and pedagogical theories?

Pedagogy is a high-stakes game, filled with contemplation, emotions, and actions. Every cup of coffee, book, or bicycle represents the efforts and results of our ancestors, transferring knowledge to the next generation.

Pedagogy in Our Complex World

We live in a complicated era. Our collective memories, experiences, stories, and imaginations constantly shape our thoughts, feelings, and actions. The pedagogical process supports the brain's encoding of knowledge, leading to survival, productivity, and cultural development.

Despite all this complexity, our historical, social, and cultural systems for pedagogical knowledge transfer work quite well. They weave our lives together, bridging individual experiences and communal understanding.

Pedagogy's Role in the Information Age

The purpose of examining contemporary issues in the knowledge and information society is to present the world from a pedagogue's perspective. We must recognize the relevance of various pedagogical missions, be aware of current challenges, and maintain a critical stance toward society's assumptions (Nesser, 2012).

As we transitioned from hunting, agriculture, industry, and information societies, tools like bows, plows, steam engines, and computers shaped our needs, motives, goals, and behaviors (Grönholm 1984; Tengström 1987). These transitions created possibilities and threats that required concrete actions.

Embracing Pedagogy with Open Hearts and Minds

The world of pedagogy is not merely an intellectual exercise; it's a part of our very essence. As a social pedagogue, my understanding of this field is both professional and deeply personal. I see the pedagogical experiences that surround each individual as something we are all capable of categorizing, ranking, and evaluating.

Our engagement with pedagogy transcends simple definitions and enters the realm of equal encounters, dialogic exchange, and constructive understanding. It empowers us to pay attention to, challenge, and liberate one another.

Let's embrace pedagogy as a vital resource for individual learning and collective growth. Let's learn to appreciate its multifaceted nature and cherish its relevance in our lives.

Shaping Futures and Fostering Wellbeing

I deeply understand the intricacies of modern education. The role of social pedagogy in schools is more vital than ever in our rapidly changing world, where it acts as a critical link between education, community, personal growth, and mental well-being.

School: A Second Home for Children

According to Berglund (2000), the school serves as a second home for children, where young minds are nurtured and shaped. The experiences they gain during their school years significantly impact their adult lives.

The school environment plays a vital role in creating identity and forming relationships with classmates, both during school hours and during leisure time.

Absence from school has immediate consequences and difficulties for the student. Missed physical attendance during classes results in a lack of education, impacting the student's active participation in studies, and social, and professional life. Increased presence in school enhances opportunities for both the student and society. Timely interventions to reduce absenteeism can minimize exclusion and support participation (SOU 2016:94).

Social Pedagogy: An Uncharted Terrain in Schools

Eriksson & Markström (2000) emphasize that a social pedagogical approach aims at human life improvement on both personal and structural levels. However, social pedagogy remains an unexplored subject in the school world, leading to misunderstandings about its significance within the educational system (Cederlund & Berglund, 2017).

Alvarsson (2018) highlights the urgent need for employing social pedagogues in schools, such as in Västerviks municipality. Still, the proposal was rejected by the Children and Education Committee. The argument for the need centered on proper treatment of students with social problems, and how easing the learning environment would be beneficial for both students and teachers.

Addressing Mental Health and Socioeconomic Challenges

Reports like the one from 2017 reveal problems surrounding mental health and stress that have escalated among students. The report also emphasizes the importance of belonging in school, addressing students who are socioeconomically disadvantaged or non-Swedish-born.

The role of student health is to lift up and cater to students' varied needs, but the report highlights shortcomings in this area. Collaboration between different professions, especially with student health, is emphasized as fundamental for a successful approach to supporting students.

Emphasizing Community and Individuality

By employing a social pedagogical approach, opportunities arise for better living conditions for individuals in society with special needs. Eriksson & Markström (2000) stress the importance of recognizing and respecting human differences, focusing on individualization. Community and an appropriate social pedagogical approach are essential in working with people to foster and maintain community.

The focus of the school, as illustrated in the Swedish School Law (2010:800), is to promote all children's development and learning and foster a lifelong love of learning. The law emphasizes the need to cater to the different needs of children and students, supporting their development as active, creative, competent, and responsible individuals.

Embracing Social Pedagogy in Schools

Social pedagogy plays a crucial role in enhancing the school environment, allowing educators and professionals to recognize and nurture individual strengths. Emphasizing community, belonging, equality, and participation, social pedagogy helps shape future citizens while promoting well-being.

The growing pressures on our children necessitate a compassionate and understanding approach. As a mother and social pedagogue, I wholeheartedly advocate for the integration of social pedagogy into our schools, as it not only enhances learning but fosters a sense of community, empathy, and resilience in our children.

A Reflection on Inclusive Education and Support Strategies

I bring forward a heartfelt perspective not only from my professional insights but also as a parent who understands the emotional intricacies involved in supporting children, especially those with specific needs such as NDD (Neurodevelopmental Disorders). This article aims to unfold the layers of the pedagogical landscape and propose integrated approaches to fostering a fair and supportive educational environment for every child.

1. The Changing Role of Pedagogues

A. The Complexities of Modern Education According to Normell (2002), the changing societal dynamics have made the role of pedagogues more challenging. Schools often witness disorderly behavior, and educators find themselves acting as mediators and counselors without proper training. Much of their time is consumed in conflict resolution, necessitating proper support and guidance to perform their roles professionally.

B. The Need for an Inclusive Approach Andersson (2004) emphasizes that children come to school with diverse backgrounds and needs. The current school system may not suit all, and it becomes a challenge to provide tailored support to every child. There's an urgent call for a fair school system where resources are distributed according to each child's needs, fostering a secure and accommodating environment.

2. The Inclusion vs. Specialized Support Debate

A. The Struggles of Inclusion Haug (1998) notes that while Sweden aimed to create a school for all, reaching the ideal of full inclusion requires more than just relocating students. There's a risk that inclusion may lead to obscurity and a lack of individual adaptation.

B. Specialized Support Groups Two main reasons are given for moving students in need of special support to smaller groups: to help the child and to preserve the class environment. While there are benefits such as individualized attention, there are also potential stigmas and isolation challenges to consider.

3. Strategies for Success

A. The Motivated Conversation Lundgren and Lökholm (2006) stress the importance of non-authoritative dialogue between the student and teacher to motivate behavior change. This process fosters self-awareness and empowers the student to take control.

B. Cognitive Behavioral Therapy (KBT) Schools like Avesta have adopted KBT, working with school groups to provide emotional support, enabling individuals to manage their thoughts and feelings.

C. Addressing Concentration Difficulties Kadesjö (2001) highlights the need for considerable support for children with concentration difficulties, recognizing their underlying social contexts and implementing strategies to improve learning experiences.

D. Aligning with Educational Plans Aligning teaching with individual needs, as stipulated in Lpfö 98 and Lpo 94, can ensure that each child receives the attention and support they require.

An Integrated Vision for the Future

Children's education is an ever-evolving domain that requires a flexible, empathetic, and structured approach. Through concerted efforts and strategies that honor the unique needs and potentials of each child, educators, parents, and communities can co-create an empowering landscape that nurtures the minds and hearts of the next generation.

Human Connection in School Environments

In the bustling corridors of schools, social pedagogy is the silent yet vital force that knits the fabric of a thriving, compassionate community. I am moved to share with you how this multifaceted field is not only transforming education but also resonating within our family lives.

Social pedagogy: the art of being human

Based on the insights of Larrison & Korr (2013), social pedagogy is rooted in theory and knowledge. But more than that, it emphasizes the human aspect of the profession — the unique blend of individual development, approach, empathy, and personal values that social pedagogues carry. The success of working with people, according to these authors, is not just in academic knowledge but also in the understanding of the personal impact of one's actions.

Relational competence: the heartbeat of interaction

Aspelin (2015) throws light on the concept of relational competence — the ability to connect with others. This includes qualities such as respect, acknowledgment, trust, and care. The way professionals meet the individual needs of students, support, motivate, and activate them, leads to positive and healthy relationships. This more intimate approach strengthens relationships and enables change.

Social pedagogy in schools: a Pan-European perspective

In the realm of education, social pedagogy finds prominence in Europe, with countries like the UK heralding the message that "every child counts." Kyriacou (2009) emphasizes five key aspects: students' well-being, social and academic learning, care, inclusion, and socialization. The focus is on confirming and enhancing students' self-image and confidence, thereby fostering a more independent and resilient individual.

The complex landscape: challenges and adaptability

Ucar (2013) underscores the complexity of social pedagogy as a subject and emphasizes that the results are not the same for every individual. The focus should be on the process and the path to the goal rather than the goal itself. Adaptability and flexibility are paramount.

Conclusion: an unfolding journey

Social pedagogy is more than a field of study or professional endeavor. It's an intricate dance of empathy, understanding, creativity, and resilience. From the classrooms to the home, the principles of social pedagogy are universal, transcending boundaries and transforming lives. In the words of Eriksson-Sjöö (2011), the goal is not just to meet targets but to engage in actions and processes that lead to individual development.

The dance of social pedagogy continues to evolve, and I am humbled to be a part of this journey. As I weave these principles into my professional work and my parenting, I realize that our shared humanity is the song that guides us. Your experiences and insights are a vital part of this conversation, and I invite you to join me in exploring this compassionate pathway toward a more empathetic world.

The Role of Social Pedagogy in Enhancing Multicultural Education

I've navigated the rich tapestry of diversity within preschools and schools. My professional journey has allowed me to explore the significance of embracing various cultures, languages, and traditions. This article will delve into the critical role that intercultural pedagogy plays in fostering an inclusive environment that recognizes and celebrates diversity.

Diversity in Schools and Society: A Social Pedagogue's Perspective

Historically, there has been a tendency to focus on the majority culture in Sweden. However, studies by scholars such as Lorentz (2007), Bozarslan (2001), and Ljungberg (2005) reveal that diverse areas are often portrayed with an oversimplified view in mass media.

In many schools, the richness of diverse cultural backgrounds is often overshadowed by traditional teaching methodologies. Although students come from various backgrounds, these diverse perspectives may not be reflected in school operations or teaching methods.

Embracing Diversity: Challenges and Opportunities

Living in a globalized society means that cultural diversity is an integral part of our daily lives. However, emphasizing our differences can sometimes overshadow the shared human experience. Addressing this challenge is crucial for promoting a culture that values diversity and encourages understanding and inclusivity.

An Inclusive Approach: The Way Forward

Intercultural pedagogy offers a promising path to embracing diversity in education. This approach promotes learning, teaching, and socialization within a multicultural context, enhancing understanding and communication between people from various cultural backgrounds.

By equipping educators with the skills to recognize how cultural factors affect individual development and learning, intercultural pedagogy can play a vital role in creating a genuinely inclusive environment that celebrates diversity in all its forms.

Conclusion: Building a Society that Values Diversity

As a Social Pedagogue, recognizing and celebrating diversity is not just an abstract concept; it's an essential part of my profession. By actively engaging with diverse cultures, traditions, and perspectives, we can foster an inclusive society that values every individual's unique contribution.

Through intercultural pedagogy, we can look beyond surface differences, build bridges between various cultural backgrounds, and make our schools, communities, and society more inclusive, understanding, and compassionate.

Navigating Classroom Conflicts

I understand the intricacies of managing conflicts in school settings. The school is a vibrant meeting place where diverse cultures converge, interacting in a common environment and forming countless relationships that may otherwise never occur outside school boundaries. It's no surprise, therefore, that conflicts arise, potentially leading to an unsafe environment that negatively affects students' learning experience.

School Conflicts and the Pedagogue's Role

The pedagogue holds the responsibility to cultivate a positive synergy between students and develop an effective learning environment. This role inevitably encompasses sound conflict management. Conflicts between students often consume a significant portion of a pedagogue's day, with media painting a critical image of how different conflicts are handled by educators and school management.

The unpredictability of conflicts, their situational nature, and their potential to arise anytime make conflict management challenging. As educators, we must be flexible and prepared to resolve conflicts in a professional manner. We require a profound understanding of how students perceive conflicts and how to best prevent and counteract disagreements.

Understanding Conflicts

To understand respondents' views on conflicts, we need to clarify and explain the meaning of conflict itself. Conflicts, being part of daily life, have always existed and will continue to exist. However, the approach toward conflicts and their management is shaped by societal norms and values. From a historical perspective, conflict management in schools has evolved from the authoritarian nature of the 19th century, where physical punishment was a common resolution method, to a more empathetic approach that acknowledges psychosocial factors as potential causes for conflicts.

A 'conflict' in a school setting could refer to disagreement over objects, rights, or decision-making authority. Over the decades, the perception of conflict has expanded to include internal conflicts within an individual and within an organization. Current conflict management research in schools aligns with this evolved understanding.

Conflict Types and Emotional Underpinnings

Conflicts can be intrapersonal (occurring within an individual), interpersonal (between people), or systemic (arising when differing norms and values within an organization are incompatible). Understanding these conflict types is critical for developing comprehensive conflict management strategies.

Despite their distinct types, conflicts essentially revolve around emotions. The discomfort that conflicts evoke is due to societal norms that favor intellect over emotions. High emotions, when expressed in conflicts, often divert the focus from the actual cause of the conflict to the emotions displayed, altering the interpretation and management of the conflict. Recognizing these emotional aspects and behavior patterns is crucial for effective conflict management.

The Power of Constructive Conflict Resolution

Conflict, if not constructively resolved, does not promote a conducive learning environment. Constructive conflict management, however, fosters students' cognitive, emotional, and social development and should be an integral part of teaching, enabling students to develop effective strategies.

Conflicts form a considerable part of students' everyday life and influence their learning process. As pedagogues, our ability to handle school conflicts is essential for our professional role. The ultimate aim is to promote an understanding of conflict not as an impediment, but as an opportunity for learning, growth, and empathy, shaping our students into well-rounded individuals.

Neurodevelopmental Disorders: A Journey of Understanding and Support

I recently read a fascinating article "More knowledge is needed about the girls" by Mats Jansson in the magazine Autism, issue 4, 2020. The article, based on an interview with Maria Bühler, a licensed psychologist and specialist in neuropsychology, provides valuable insights into the diagnosis and support of girls with neurodevelopmental disorders (NDD) like autism and ADHD.

Maria, the author of "Girls with Autism and ADHD: A Guidebook for Parents and Professionals," explains that there's a critical lack of information about NDD diagnoses in girls in Sweden. She mentions that emotional difficulties in girls are often attributed to an unstable "emotional level" rather than a neuropsychiatric disorder, diverting focus from the core issues at hand.

My journey in understanding NDD is both professional and personal. My youngest son was diagnosed with language difficulties disorder at the age of four. Together with preschool educators, special educators, speech therapists, and psychologists, we have worked relentlessly for my son's development.

A short period of our journey was tough, with suspicions of autism hovering around us. However, the special educator insisted on providing him with the necessary help and support. We observed his progress before considering a referral to Child and Youth Psychiatry. For a year, my son was part of a small group of five children in preschool, under the care of two educators and a special educator who actively engaged with the children's deficiencies.

The last meeting with the special educator brought us wonderful news. My son's treatment plan had concluded as he was now on par with other children of his age. He had minor language deficiencies, but nothing that required special treatment. The only continuity required was with the speech therapist.

Through my journey, I found that there are other reasons behind behavioral disorders beyond NDD diagnoses. Dyslexia, language, or hearing difficulties can not only cause these but can also affect children who have an NDD diagnosis.

Understanding the challenges that children with NDD diagnoses face, and the strain it can put on teachers and educators, is vital. But these challenges also present opportunities to find new ways to educate and manage students successfully.

The key lies in understanding the world from their perspective. I recommend the book "Autism and ADHD in High School", which provides a comprehensive insight into this. The book also mentions young people sharing their school experiences and biggest challenges, which is another resource that paints a vivid picture of the struggle these children face.

Growing up with an NDD disorder can be frustrating and challenging. But the problem is not the diagnosis — it's the lack of understanding and acceptance, and the inability to adapt teaching and learning strategies that match these children's unique needs.

With recent studies revealing an increase in ADHD diagnoses in adults in Sweden, it's more crucial than ever to open dialogues about these conditions in schools. As we create more supportive environments for these children, we allow them to grow into adults who understand and manage their conditions effectively, leading to better relationships, improved self-esteem, and successful careers.

I chose the social pedagogue program to help children with learning difficulties/NDD diagnoses, driven by a strong motivation from my personal experiences. I encourage open dialogues and a keen interest in understanding each child's unique needs — because everyone deserves a chance to flourish in their own way.

From the Roots of Reggio Emilia

Bridging knowledge gaps through the philosophy of Loris Malaguzzi

Let me take you on a journey to my intellectual and personal world. A world with the roots of social pedagogy, drawing inspiration from the renowned Italian psychologist and elementary school teacher Loris Malaguzzi (1921–1994) and his profound impact on the Reggio Emilia philosophy. With my experiences and insights, I invite you to explore the transformative power of this approach, as it resonates deeply within my work and personal growth.

The philosophy

Malaguzzi's philosophy was born as a response to the fascist ideologies of war-torn Italy, when he, along with a group of women, established a preschool in his hometown. Over three decades, he became the guiding force behind Reggio Emilia's municipal childcare, perceiving education as a living idea that emerges from children's thoughts and the current context (Wallin, 2001). Malaguzzi drew inspiration from the thinking of several educators and philosophers, including Maria Montessori, Piaget, Marx, Freinet, and Vygotsky (Brulin & Emriksson, 2005).

Reggio Emilia, often referred to as the province in the Emilia-Romagna region, holds a special place in the realm of pedagogical philosophy. The city of Reggio Emilia itself, with around 165,000 inhabitants, has gained international recognition for the educational philosophy that emerged in the aftermath of World War II. This philosophy has come to be known as "Reggio Emilia," named after the city itself (Wallin, 2001).

Despite the absence of original literature, Malaguzzi penned a significant document titled "A Paper for Three Rights" a year before his passing in 1993. In this document, he articulated the rights of children, educators, and parents, emphasizing that children have the right to be the protagonists of their individual, civic, legal, and social rights. These rights are fostered through relationships with both children and adults. Malaguzzi also stressed the importance of collaboration between preschool and home, believing it provides children with a sense of security and equilibrium. He described children's discussions as a lantern guiding the search for knowledge. Their thoughts, interests, and ideas should shape the pedagogical work and planning (Jonstoij & Tolgraven, 2001).

Moreover, Malaguzzi recognized the interconnectivity of human beings and their context. He believed that the brain develops when it is actively engaged. A rich childhood that encourages problem-solving, choice, and the expression of a hundred languages influences brain development. The brain's hundred languages constantly collaborate. This contrasts with the foundation of Swedish elementary education, established in 1842, where rote memorization took precedence over understanding (Wallin, 2001).

Malaguzzi's famous poem "The Hundred Languages" beautifully encapsulates his view of children and their learning. It permeates much of the literature we have studied:

A child is made of a hundred.

The child has a hundred languages,

a hundred hands,

a hundred thoughts,

a hundred ways of thinking, of playing, of speaking.

A hundred always a hundred...

Ways of listening, of marveling, of loving,

a hundred joys for singing and understanding.

A hundred worlds to discover, a hundred worlds to dream.

A child has a hundred languages (and a hundred hundred hundred more), but they steal ninety-nine.

The school and the culture separate the head from the body.

They tell the child: To think without hands, to do without the head, to listen and not to speak, to understand without joy, to love and to marvel only at Easter and Christmas.

They tell the child: To discover the world already there and of the hundred they steal ninety-nine.

They tell the child: That work and play, reality and fantasy, science and imagination, sky and earth, reason and dream are things that do not belong together.

And thus they tell the child that the hundred is not there.

The child says: No way. The hundred is there.

Through this poignant poem, Malaguzzi expressed his opposition to the dominant perspectives on children and their learning (Dahlberg & Göthsson, 2005). A hundred languages metaphorically represent the diverse means of expression that humans possess to understand the world around them (Jonstoij & Tolgraven, 2001). He emphasized the importance of nurturing children's belief in their abilities and providing them with educational experiences that allow them to express themselves through these hundred languages.

The Mindset

Reggio Emilia is not a method but a mindset, devoid of predefined models to follow. Its philosophy is rooted in a democratic understanding of humanity, where communication plays a pivotal role (Gedin & Sjöblom, 1995). Reggio Emilia's philosophical pedagogy embodies a social constructivist perspective, viewing knowledge as something co-created through interactions with others. Within this framework, knowledge is intertwined with sensory and embodied experiences, rejecting the separation of facts and imagination (Jonstoij & Tolgraven, 2001). While not explicitly stated, many other pedagogical authors have also highlighted aspects central to Reggio Emilia's approach.

Carlgren (1992) emphasizes that knowledge is constructed by the individual, influenced by space, time, cultural and linguistic contexts, with an individual's experiences shaping their understanding in the present moment. Additionally, the development of comprehension and thought patterns is intrinsically connected to the subject matter itself.

In Reggio Emilia's philosophy, one of the most prominent tenets regarding children's learning is that it is ever-changing and evolving. It is the pedagogist's and educators' responsibility to plan and contemplate, ensuring that the educational environment progresses in step with society. Reggio Emilia emphasizes the municipality's or city's accountability for young children's learning, valuing their rights and cherishing their childhood. It does not present a ready-made template but rather relies on guiding principles (Phillips, 2001). In our study, we will focus on three key aspects that are particularly relevant.

1. Approach

Each individual holds their perspective on children and their understanding, shaping their view of what children are and can be. In Swedish preschools, various theoretical perspectives can be discerned, with the most dominant being psychological. However, international research indicates an ongoing paradigm shift in understanding children. The term "the competent child" is becoming increasingly common, reflecting a shift from perceiving children as fragile and in need of help to seeing them as communicative and capable beings. Reggio Emilia has, from the beginning, explored various pedagogical approaches to gain a deeper understanding of their perspective (Jonstoij & Tolgraven, 2001). Understanding children requires getting to know their world. We cannot face modern children and perceive them as a child from a bygone era (Gedin & Sjöblom, 1995). Malaguzzi argued that we must make children's worlds visible by showing genuine interest. A fundamental aspect of Reggio Emilia is viewing each child as unique and recognizing that the child is the protagonist in their development. Malaguzzi described three different perspectives on children:

2. Viewing the child as passive, not active

The child observes adults and then replicates their knowledge. Although this perspective is rare in theory, it is often noticeable in practice. b. Believing that the child requires stimulation from adults to develop. This child is not independent in their learning, and adults must take an active role. Malaguzzi referred to this as a "wakeful but impoverished child" (Gedin & Sjöblom, 1995). c. Aligning with the Reggio Emilia approach, the child creates their knowledge. This child wants to learn, grow, and know. They also need an adult who protects them as a co-creator, someone with whom they can communicate, exchange thoughts, and transcend boundaries. It is essential to help children develop a strong sense of self while emphasizing social connections and a sense of belonging (Gedin & Sjöblom, 1995). Jonstoij & Tolgraven (2001) also underscore the importance of learning as a two-way communication process, where dialogue between children and adults facilitates learning.

3. The educator's attitude towards children plays a crucial role in their approach

Children's motivation to learn is influenced by the educator's perspective on learning, their understanding of children, and the feedback and encouragement they provide. This reciprocal interaction affects children's sense of well-being, motivation, and desire to learn (Giota, 2001).

4. Environment

In Reggio Emilia's philosophy, the environment serves as a pedagogue that stimulates and inspires children (Wallin, 2001). The environment should challenge and encourage children in their thoughts and imaginations (Wallin, 2001). Children acquire knowledge through their interactions with their surroundings. The design of the educational environment significantly impacts children's learning, to the extent that the environment is equated with a pedagogue. The physical environment of the classroom should be dynamic, allowing children to actively participate in its design. Children should have the freedom to rearrange and partition spaces according to their activities. Furthermore, they should have the opportunity for personal space.

5. Reggio Emilia places importance on technology as an integral part of society

In today's world, computers are ubiquitous. Therefore, it is appropriate for children to have access to computers in preschool. The computers should be accessible to children without requiring adult supervision, allowing them to engage spontaneously. Another characteristic of Reggio Emilia-inspired preschools is the presence of an atelier (Wallin, 2001). Located behind a glass wall on the premises, the atelier is a workshop connected to all the classrooms in Reggio Emilia's preschools. It contains various tools and materials used by both children and adults (Abbott & Nuthbrown, 2005). According to Häikiö (2007), the atelier offers diverse materials for children to explore. It is a space for experimentation and laboratory work, where children can utilize different materials and forms of expression. Mirrors, in various forms, are also common in Reggio Emilia-inspired preschools. They encourage children to observe themselves and reflect upon their observations (Nuthbrown, 2005).

6. Pedagogy-Child Relationship:

The educator's approach to children supersedes the specific teaching methods employed. Therefore, educators often organize activities using long-term projects, allowing children to work in small groups on topics and themes brimming with energy that tap into their creativity and curiosity. The educator's role here differs from that of a traditional teacher, as the focus lies on the process rather than the result. They value children's theories and pose challenges that propel learning forward. The educator's beliefs about a child's abilities influence what the children can achieve, making it crucial to adopt an approach that believes in children's capabilities rather than perceiving age as a hindrance to their potential (Jonstoij & Tolgraven, 2001). Vygotsky argued that children guided by adults or peers can accomplish more than they can on their own. Cooperation with adults and peers elevates children to higher levels, fostering motivation and social skills. Children must learn to collaborate (Vygotsky, 1995). Pramling and Doverborg (1995) also highlight how diverse thinking within a group of children fosters learning among them. Differences should be seen as opportunities, rather than obstacles, within the pedagogical work. Children's thoughts should not be corrected but developed into a way of thinking and relating to oneself and the surrounding world. Differences are valued and serve as a positive and challenging foundation for educational work. True discussions emerge from diverse opinions. The Reggio Emilia philosophy emphasizes maintaining a critical mindset and embracing new thoughts and perspectives, as there are no absolute truths but a continuous search for understanding (Wallin, 2001).

Parts of the aforementioned concepts are mirrored in the Swedish preschool curriculum, where learning is based on interactions between adults and children, as well as children learning from one another. The group of children should be viewed as a crucial and active part of development and learning. Preschool should support children in developing a positive self-perception as learners and creators. They should be helped to believe in their capacity for independent thinking, action, movement, and learning, encompassing various aspects such as intellectual, linguistic, ethical, practical, sensory, and aesthetic (Lpfö98).

Final thoughts

In conclusion, the Reggio Emilia philosophy intertwines the transformative power of children's voices, the dynamic educational environment, and the nurturing pedagogical relationships to create a rich and empowering learning experience. By embracing this social pedagogy, we open the door to a world where children are valued as active participants, where their thoughts and expressions are cherished, and where their curiosity is cultivated to shape the future.

Unlocking the Power of Critical Thinking in Education: A Swedish Perspective

In this context, the field of social pedagogy is uniquely poised to contribute to the ongoing discourse. In Sweden, as in many other countries, social pedagogy emphasizes a holistic approach to education, one that integrates learning with the development of social skills and the strengthening of community bonds. It encourages an understanding of education that extends beyond mere academic proficiency or vocational training, emphasizing instead the development of the whole person — physically, socially, emotionally, and intellectually.

From a social pedagogy perspective, knowledge is not just about the accumulation of facts, but about fostering critical thinking, facilitating social engagement, and nurturing empathy and respect for diversity. It is about creating spaces for dialogue and collaboration, where individuals can learn from one another, challenge prevailing perspectives, and contribute to a more inclusive, equitable, and democratic society.

As we move further into the 21st century, we have the opportunity to reconceptualize our understanding of knowledge and its role in society. Through social pedagogy, we can emphasize the importance of knowledge as a tool not only for individual advancement but also for social cohesion, community building, and the promotion of democratic values. By doing so, we can help shape a future of education that is responsive to our changing world and that continues to uphold the values that make our society strong.

Knowledge and Education

Knowledge can be regarded as a pathway for individuals to align with their surroundings and the norms and values ingrained in society. An integral part of the discourse around the concept of knowledge is the practice of critical thinking, which is increasingly emphasized in modern school culture.

In the context of Swedish education, critical thinking serves as a guide at all levels. It's based on the recognition that our understanding of knowledge and information is inherently incomplete. Therefore, critical thinking becomes an essential tool with two facets — discovery and proof — to aid in the advancement of our cognitive abilities (Eriksson, 2018).

The educators' role

The anticipation of formal education is that it will result in knowledge, skills, and values. Consequently, the contents of education require continual revision in response to the evolution of knowledge and changes in values.

The role of the educator entails the ability to foster an understanding of what qualifies as knowledge and to identify analytical tools to evaluate the qualities of the knowledge they impart from written curricula to practical teaching.

Education, in the contemporary academic discourse, is perceived as an ongoing construction that is subject to regular discussions and debates, prompted by societal demands for the ability to build knowledge without strictly defined boundaries across different quantities of knowledge, like subjects, material, and elements.

Critical thinking in Pedagogy

Schools serve society and its specific interests. Their mission is twofold — a knowledge-related and a democracy-related component. Critical thinking naturally has a place in this discourse, connecting knowledge and learning.

The complexity of critical thinking is evident in its significance for society and education. It is upheld as an innate characteristic of a democratic citizen and an expected outcome of pedagogical contexts (Poporov, 2016). The ability of schools to establish abstract facts in students is crucial, as it allows students to apply and test these facts against concrete events in the external world.

Indeed, critical thinking is a precondition for students' ability to navigate a changing world teeming with a continuous flow of information. Their capacity to apply a critical approach to their lived experiences depends on an education that equips them with resources to assess information and helps them develop an understanding of their environment.

The "School for Education"

Critical thinking must be identified as a perennial topic, which teachers must frequently discuss among themselves and with their students. It needs to be continually discussed in the educational political context and nuanced in societal debates.

The concept of knowledge and how it can/should be perceived in a didactic context sets a normative basis for organizing student learning. Society's perception of what constitutes knowledge shapes each school system and permeates the theoretical content of the curriculum.

The "School for Education" committee report (SOU 1992:94) presents a contemporary didactic paradigm concerning the connection between knowledge and learning. It adds a normative basis for organizing student learning, preparing the groundwork for the modern understanding of knowledge in Swedish schools from the mid-1990s and beyond.

Final thoughts

In line with the principles of social pedagogy, it is also essential to consider the broader, often overlooked aspects of education. The school, beyond being an academic institution, is also a hub for social learning and interaction, where students learn to navigate social relationships, deal with conflicts, respect diversity, and understand the nuances of being a part of a larger community, is "one of the supporting foundations for societal stability and development"(Bergh, 2012).

This perspective also underscores the importance of educators as more than transmitters of academic knowledge. Teachers, through their interactions and relationships with students, contribute significantly to their social development and moral understanding. They model critical thinking, empathy, conflict resolution, and many other valuable life skills that students will carry with them into adulthood.

Moreover, with the increasing digitalization of our society, it's crucial that we equip students with the knowledge and critical thinking skills necessary to navigate the digital landscape responsibly and effectively. This includes not only technical skills but also an understanding of digital citizenship, online safety, and the ethical use of digital technology.

In conclusion, while academic knowledge and critical thinking skills are undeniably important, a truly well-rounded education is one that also prioritizes social and emotional learning, digital literacy, and the development of the whole person. A future-focused approach to education, informed by social pedagogy, can help us achieve this.

Children and Learning: A Comparative Analysis of Theoretical Approaches

In my pursuit to understand the nuances of child development and learning, it is essential to delve into diverse theoretical frameworks. As a social pedagogue, I aim to provide you with an understanding of these theories and their impact on the learning process, particularly focusing on children with Autism.

Behaviorism

Behaviorism, originating from the works of Russian physiologist and psychologist Ivan Pavlov (1849-1936) and later developed by American psychologist B.F. Skinner (1904-1990), posits that our actions are guided by the consequences of similar previous actions. In the behaviorist perspective, learning is defined as a change in observable behavior, disregarding cognitive activities like thoughts and reflections as they are unobservable.

Cognitivism

In contrast, Cognitivism, often linked to Swiss researcher Jean Piaget (1896-1980), shifts its interest to the cognitive abilities and mental processes of individuals. Underlying this approach is the constructivist perspective which posits that individuals construct their understanding of the world through their activities.

The Sociocultural Theory

The Sociocultural perspective, rooted in the work of Russian psychologist Lev Vygotsky (1896-1934), emphasizes the role of social interactions and cultural tools in shaping an individual's development and learning.

Understanding these theories provides valuable insights into the learning process of children with autism. From a Behaviorist perspective, the adult is responsible for a child's learning. However, from a Cognitivist/Constructivist standpoint, a child has an intrinsic motivation to seek knowledge, and from a Sociocultural perspective, the environment plays a crucial role in a child's learning.

My perspective on children with autism and learning is based on an integrated approach, incorporating the Sociocultural perspective and contemporary cognitive research. I believe it is crucial to view each child with autism as a unique individual, acknowledging their strengths, interests, and characteristics. In designing an educational plan, the child's individual cognitive profile, interests, and learning style should be the starting point.

Final thoughts

In conclusion, the intricacies of learning theories provide us with diverse ways to understand and support the development of children. In the case of children with autism, it is essential to design an individualized plan that supports their cognitive and social development and reduces stress.

Each child's development depends on their capabilities, the extent of their disability, and the environment's ability to understand, adapt, and create learning situations. Remember, learning occurs in all natural contexts, and planned interventions should occur within a natural setting as much as possible.

Learning is a journey we undertake together — a journey of understanding, growth, and shared responsibility.

Adapting to Diverse Needs and Encouraging Learning

My life is significantly intertwined with pedagogy and its profound influence on our children's lives. Having personally committed to fostering a tolerant, inclusive educational environment, I have a keen interest in pedagogical methods and the lasting impact they have on students.

The teaching approach taken by a school forms the foundation for how its students perform and grow. My experiences, both professionally and as a parent, echo the research findings that suggest students excel in smaller class sizes. Furthermore, the union of these smaller classes with teachers who are comprehensively competent, preferably equipped with special education skills, sets the stage for a more inclusive, beneficial learning experience (Persson, 1998).

The goal is to create a nurturing environment where differences in knowledge and performance levels are not only accepted but also celebrated. In such settings, every student is given a chance to meet their potential and flourish, regardless of their starting point. This inclusive approach is particularly beneficial for students who may start with lower performance levels, as they thrive more than they would in a homogeneous knowledge group (Williams, Pramling Samuelsson, 2000).

The inclusive school

In an inclusive school, addressing the varied needs of students requires more resources, particularly more adults and smaller student groups (Johansson, 2000). This aspect is fundamental to the Salamanca Declaration, which emphasizes establishing an inclusive learning environment and requires the education system to accommodate equal education for all.

Strategies need to be adapted to individuals rather than an entire class to benefit all students. By doing this, negative attitudes toward differences decrease, demonstrating the importance of social interaction in an inclusive school (Persson, 2007). The school must ensure conducive conditions for all students' learning, which involves understanding individual students' varying conditions and recognizing that different approaches, methods, and readings are needed to support students' learning (Gadler, 2011).

The Impact of Teaching Approach on Students with Special Needs

A key point for teachers is understanding that students with ADHD and Asperger's can, once they start their work, become overexcited and find it difficult to manage this intensity. Teachers, therefore, need to instruct in a manner that helps the student manage their impulses with the teacher's signs and support (Abrahamsson, 2010).

Indeed, modern schools often struggle with budget cuts that significantly impact resources available for supportive interventions. These cuts harshly affect students with varying types of issues (Persson, 1998). According to Persson (1998), the teaching provided in schools and by individual teachers cannot reach all students with such varied needs. Special educational efforts represent the only opportunity for teachers to have a reasonable chance of shaping the teaching and meeting the demands of the curriculum.

Motivation for Learning: A Key Aspect in Teaching

Encouraging students' motivation for learning is achieved by making them feel successful at tasks and giving them opportunities to showcase their knowledge to others (Abrahamsson, 2010). This aspect should apply to all students. However, it becomes challenging for students with behavioral disorders or social problems to display their knowledge and feel successful in a combined class where disjunctive teaching is used.

Motivation is not an inherent quality of an individual but is a result of the experiences one has had and the treatment received (Jenner, 2004). Therefore, it becomes the teacher's responsibility to respond and encourage students based on their experiences so that motivation can arise. The motivating factors for students with special needs can differ significantly from those of typical students. A quieter environment, fewer choices, and rewards often benefit students with special needs (Abrahamsson, 2010).

Final thoughts

With my journey as a Social Pedagogue and mother of three boys at the heart of my reflections, I firmly believe in the transformative power of an inclusive educational landscape. We must strive to evolve beyond traditional teaching paradigms and adopt approaches that acknowledge and respect the beautiful diversity of our student population.

By shifting the teaching paradigm from a purely sociocultural approach to one that incorporates behavioral aspects, we can facilitate a more inclusive school environment. This dynamic model seeks to accommodate the multifaceted needs of all learners and promotes motivation and success among students with diverse needs.

As a norm-critical pedagogue, I have witnessed firsthand how this shift can open up worlds of opportunity, challenging ingrained norms and offering a platform where every child, no matter their background or learning style, can thrive. As a mother, I see the undeniable value in nurturing our children to be understanding, inclusive individuals who appreciate diversity.

In closing, I would like to thank you for joining me in this exploration of pedagogical methods and their impacts. It is my deepest hope that our collective efforts will contribute to a more tolerant, inclusive education and world. Let us continue this conversation and strive together for a future where every child finds their place in the learning landscape.

The Power of Waldorf Pedagogy: Nurturing the Holistic Development of a Child

The early years of our lives are a crucial time for personal development. As a passionate student of Waldorf pedagogy, I've had the unique opportunity to witness how this method facilitates a child's development by aligning it with nature's rhythms and fostering holistic growth.

First Seven-Year Period: "The World is Good"

In Waldorf pedagogy, the first seven-year period of a child's life is critical.

This is the stage where children develop their will and learn through imitation, soaking in everything from their surroundings. Active and positive role models are key, providing nourishment to the body, soul, play, and learning. The main pedagogical summary of this period is "The world is good". Here, the adults around the child have the mission of fostering a sense of goodness and security in the world around them.

In simple terms, the adult becomes the child's world. Through play, the child begins to understand and experience the physical world. Toys should be simple and made from natural materials, allowing the child to feel and perceive the structure, scent, weight, color, and form.

Second Seven-Year Period: "The World is Beautiful"

From school readiness until puberty, the teacher primarily works with practical subjects. The goal during this period is for the child to internalize the feeling that "The world is beautiful."

The teacher does not impose knowledge of major environmental problems or similar subjects during this period, as it may cause despair and anxiety. In this stage, the teacher acts as an authority, a role model whom students admire, respect, and trust.

Third Seven-Year Period: "The World is True"

This last school period is crucial for the child's intellectual awakening. It's a time when the teacher becomes a specialist, focusing on the development of free thought. Students are encouraged to question, explore, and think independently. This is a critical time when all threads from previous school years are tied together.

Integrating Age Groups

Integration plays a significant role in Waldorf pedagogy, unifying preschool, school, and after-school activities. However, classes are typically taught individually, with integration occurring through monthly Waldorf school festivals where students participate in a joint program displayed for all students and their parents.

The Role of a Teacher in a Waldorf School

Working in a Waldorf school requires a strong commitment to the anthroposophical philosophy that underlies this pedagogical method. Decisions are made through dialogue and consensus rather than voting, and there's no headmaster role. This results in a strong, collaborative work environment, which is invaluable in the daily pedagogical work.

Teaching Specific Subjects in the Waldorf Way

Learning is made fascinating and engaging through the teaching of specific subjects like Eurythmy, a unique form of movement that reflects the sounds and tones of language and music, Crafts, Music, and Form Drawing. Waldorf's pedagogy also utilizes an artistic approach to teaching, placing emphasis on the spoken word's human contact, substance, and intimacy over printed textbooks and technological aids.

Teaching Mathematics in the Waldorf Way

Waldorf pedagogy believes in nurturing not just the right answer in mathematics, but the entire process leading up to it. This promotes the development of logic, imagination, and precision in thinking.

National Tests

While national tests may pose a significant challenge for the Waldorf pedagogical method, which typically does not utilize tests until the ninth year, the schools have managed to conduct them successfully.

Final thoughts

In conclusion, Waldorf's pedagogy offers a unique and nurturing approach to education that is both natural and holistic. This method seeks to raise children who can confidently say that their world is good, beautiful, and true.

I hope that sharing my personal experiences and studies of the Waldorf pedagogical method will inspire you to explore this educational approach further.

Freinet Pedagogy: A Journey of Educational Transformation

I want to share a personal and heartfelt story about my journey as an educator and how the implementation of Freinet pedagogy profoundly impacted not only my professional life but also the lives of my students. This is a narrative of exploration, discovery, and transformation.

Freinet Pedagogy, coined by French pedagogue Celestin Freinet (1896–1966), is an educational methodology that emphasizes practical work, self-direction, and contact with nature and society as essential parts of the learning experience. Initially, a village schoolteacher, Freinet's works have influenced several Swedish curricula and are widely accepted by the Swedish Education Agency, Skolverket. Today, Freinet pedagogy is practiced in many countries across Europe and the world, with several independent schools in Sweden dedicated to this approach.

The Freinet School

My journey began at a Freinet school in Sweden, which is part of a network of teachers inspired by Freinet's practical work under the umbrella organization "Kooperativet Arbetets pedagogik" (The Cooperative of Pedagogy). These schools collectively work towards cultivating a learning environment that respects and promotes the individuality and creativity of each child. Freinet's Pedagogy asserts that the school should be a place of work, not a pastime. It upholds that children should be actively involved in their learning process and that the knowledge they gain should be meaningful and useful. It values hands-on experiences as essential for a child's development, as much as intellectual engagement.

The Freinet Pedagogy

Freinet pedagogy consistently encourages students to interact with the natural and social world that surrounds them. The premise is to make them realize where their work is directed, and how it can contribute to society. The goal is to develop them into independent individuals with unique identities, capable of critical thinking. At the heart of Freinet's pedagogy lies the principle of "Arbetets pedagogik", the pedagogy of work. There lies the belief in preparing children for their future lives as adults by teaching them meaningful skills that they observe adults using in society.

The Approach

The children encompass a wide range of activities like role-playing, experimenting with natural materials, and working on artistic expressions. They learn largely by practically handling reality, especially through hands-on activities. The Freinet school provides ample opportunities for children to apply theoretical knowledge practically, which includes working on crafts such as building things, sewing, painting, and weaving among other things.

These activities not only enrich motor skills and the ability to plan work, but also enhance mathematical skills (construction, calculation, geometry), language, creativity, and much more. One quote by Loris Mallaguzzi, the head of nurseries in Reggio Emilia, which deeply resonates with us is, "A child has more than a hundred languages, but is robbed of ninety-nine."

Children's Activities

Children in the Freinet school are encouraged to express themselves freely and develop their imagination and creative abilities. In all these processes, the role of the teacher or pedagogue is crucial. While they place much responsibility in the hands of the children, the ideas and direction of the work are guided by the teacher's insights. The goal is to help children actualize their possibilities and learn to take responsibility for their work.

Freinet pedagogy allows children to learn at their own pace, and adapt their learning process to suit their abilities. This approach respects individual differences and promotes a positive learning environment.

This methodology prepares children for the responsibilities of adult life and enhances their capacity to make informed decisions. Freinet believes that every individual has the right to know what they will be doing during the day. This applies to the school too. Through a posted schedule in the groups' rooms, children can always check what will happen during different times of the day and adapt their work accordingly.

The Goal

The ultimate aim is to provide children with meaningful knowledge. To strive to ensure children can see the relevance of learning a specific thing. Motivation should be immediate; learning should feel necessary now, not only for the future. Writing, for example, is a communicative act that serves to tell something, ask, narrate, or remember.

In Freinet school, writing is an important aspect, both for personal memorization and fantasy and for communicating with others. It starts as early as preschool, where children and educators evaluate their day by the educator writing down children's thoughts on flip charts. They also encourage domestic and international correspondence with other Freinet schools, providing rich opportunities to practice language and understand different living conditions — an integration of geography and social studies!

Children often publish their texts in a class magazine or on a website to share with family and friends. Sales from these publications can provide a fund the group can use for collective purchases. While the pedagogues entrust a lot of responsibility to the children and often place them in the background, it is their ideas and thoughts as educators that steer the work in the right direction. They provide support and guidance while encouraging students to take charge of their learning.

Final thoughts

Adopting Freinet's pedagogy has brought a significant transformation in the overall learning culture of our school. It has replaced passive learning with an active, engaging process, instilling a sense of responsibility and independence in our students. And as educators, it has enriched our professional lives and enabled us to contribute more meaningfully to the holistic development of our students.

My journey with Freinet pedagogy has been a transformative one, profoundly impacting the way we teach and students learn. I believe this model holds great promise in the shaping of education systems worldwide, allowing for a more inclusive, student-centered approach that nurtures not just academic skills, but also interpersonal, social, and creative abilities.

Unveiling the Depths of Psychological Treatment Methods: A Compassionate Guide to Mental Health

Imagine a world where individuals fully understand the processes behind their emotions, thoughts, behaviors and the treatments that can help in managing them. It would not only usher in a wave of awareness, but it would also erase the stigma surrounding mental health and its various treatment methods.

The world of psychological treatments encompasses a broad range of scientifically validated treatment methods that can be personalized to the unique needs of individuals. Let's delve into this enriching journey to understand these therapeutic interventions.

Psychotherapy: A Collaborative Approach to Mental Health

Psychotherapy, perhaps the most recognized form of psychological treatment, revolves around the construction of a collaborative relationship between the therapist and the client. The roles of the therapist can vary; they may be psychologists, physicians, social workers, or nurses who have undergone training in psychotherapy.

This treatment is tailored to the needs of the client, addressing various mental health conditions like depression, anxiety disorders, eating disorders, sleep difficulties, and personal crises. It also proves beneficial for individuals experiencing relationship issues.

Cognitive Behavioral Therapy: Rewiring Thoughts and Actions

Cognitive Behavioral Therapy (CBT), a widely used psychological treatment, stems from principles of learning psychology, cognitive psychology, and social psychology. It's aimed at altering how the client perceives, reacts, and relates to their inner experiences. This therapeutic approach teaches clients how to transform their thought patterns and behaviors, equipping them with tools to handle problematic situations and gradually accept their emotions and experiences.

A subtype of CBT, Trauma-Focused Cognitive Behavioral Therapy (TF-CBT), helps individuals with Post Traumatic Stress Disorder (PTSD) confront and cope with their traumatic experiences. Meanwhile, another form, known as Mindfulness-based Cognitive Therapy, integrates mindfulness practices with CBT to promote a non-judgmental understanding of thoughts, feelings, and physical sensations.

Dialectical Behavior Therapy: Managing Emotional Instability

Originally developed for suicidal and self-harming individuals with Emotionally Unstable Personality Disorder (EUPD), Dialectical Behavior Therapy (DBT) aims to reduce self-harming behaviors and other behaviors that disrupt treatment or significantly impact life quality. The long-term goal of DBT is to teach the individual to achieve emotional balance, manage daily life better, and find a meaningful existence.

ERGT and ERITA: Novel Approaches for Self-Harm Behaviors

Emotion Regulation Group Therapy (ERGT) and Emotion Regulation Individual Therapy for Adolescents (ERITA) are specifically designed to address self-harming behaviors. While ERGT focuses on enhancing emotion regulation skills in a group setting, ERITA offers individual therapy, guiding adolescents to manage intense and confusing thoughts and feelings related to self-harming behaviors.

Psychodynamic Psychotherapy: Exploring the Unconscious

Psychodynamic Psychotherapy, rooted in psychoanalysis, helps clients focus on unconscious and repressed emotions. Short-term Psychodynamic Therapy (ST-PDT) is an adaptation that emphasizes emotional expressions and addresses behavioral patterns within a limited time frame.

Mentalization-Based Therapy: Enhancing Self-Awareness

Mentalization-Based Therapy (MBT) seeks to heighten an individual's ability to mentalize — to be aware and reflect on one's thoughts, feelings, reactions, and motivations. Through this therapeutic approach, adults and adolescents with personality disorders can gradually increase their mentalization ability, gain control over their emotions, and modify their behavior.

Interpersonal Psychotherapy: Improving Relations for Better Mental Health

Interpersonal Psychotherapy (IPT) targets relational problems that contribute to mental health issues, focusing on how these problems and mental health issues reciprocally impact each other.

Each form of psychological treatment is unique, adaptable, and offers a different perspective on managing mental health. Just like all forms of care, these treatments must be tailored to the individual needs of the person receiving treatment.

As we continue to shine a light on these psychological treatments, I hope this opens doors for a more accepting, compassionate, and mentally aware society.

A Crossroads Between Behaviorist and Sociocultural Approaches

In my journey to enhance the education system, I noticed that educators often find themselves at the crossroads between traditional and modern approaches to teaching. On one hand, the behaviorist perspective, rooted in antiquity, views students as passive receivers of knowledge, with teachers adopting an authoritarian role. On the other hand, the sociocultural approach highlights the importance of interaction and social context in learning.

From the behaviorist standpoint, as outlined by Hwang & Nilsson (2011), teachers lecture, after which students work individually, often from a textbook, maintaining the same pace as their classmates. This structure instills discipline and adherence to routines and rules set by the teacher. Students learn the expected behavior and responses to different situations based on the teacher's conduct. A prime example of a theorist associated with behaviorism is B.F. Skinner. His theory focuses on socializing students into society through positive or negative reinforcement, akin to Cognitive Behavioral Therapy (CBT) often used for students with special needs associated with interaction difficulties, impulsivity, and concentration problems.

Behaviorist Teaching Methods

Teaching methods deriving from the behaviorist perspective focus on reinforcing positive behavior through reward systems like gold stars. Non-compliance or failure does not earn rewards, and there are measures to punish incorrect actions, such as the infamous "shame corner". According to Hwang and Nilsson (2011), negative reinforcement decreases the likelihood of behavior repetition by introducing unpleasant stimuli or removing desired ones. A quiet classroom, individual work without discussions, and organized workspaces minimize disruptions. Research shows that these methods are beneficial for students with conditions like ADHD and Asperger's Syndrome. Responsibility for what and how to learn is solely placed on the teacher, with the student's cultural context disregarded.

Contrary to this approach, the sociocultural perspective, pioneered by thinkers like Piaget and Vygotsky, places great emphasis on the interaction between children and adults for learning. Learning occurs in interaction with others, in the encounter between different experiences and knowledge (Williams, 2001). This perspective views individuals not only in relation to other people but also in their interaction with technology and other elements of their environment. Therefore, schools should extend beyond teaching different subjects and disciplines to reflect the prevailing societal culture the students inhabit.

Sociocultural Teaching Methods

Grounded in the sociocultural perspective, the student is seen as competent to participate in the design and content of what is to be learned. Learning should be reciprocal, with dialogues conducted on various levels and within different subjects. Moreover, students are not just learners from the teacher but also from their peers. This method views the classroom as a collective learning environment, with an emphasis on group work, common discussions, and shared responsibilities.

In light of Sweden's current national curriculum, the sociocultural teaching methods reflect the goals of fostering student influence and developing teaching based on the student's interests.

Final thoughts

As educators, understanding these perspectives helps us see that there isn't a one-size-fits-all method for teaching. Instead, it shows us the potential for synergy — the potential to merge these approaches to tailor a more inclusive, effective, and comprehensive teaching method, respecting each student's individual needs and promoting inclusivity.

A Guide to Behavioral Responses

I consider it my duty to break down complex psychological concepts into understandable terms, and in doing so, help you navigate the intricate dynamics of our everyday lives. Today, let's explore the concepts of habituation and sensitization, two behavioral responses that immensely shape how we interact with our surroundings.

Habituation: A Friend in Disguise

Imagine you have just moved into a new apartment. As night falls, and you turn off the lights for the first sleep in your new home, you start to notice a symphony of sounds that you hadn't paid attention to during the day — the irritating hum of the radiator, the jolt of surprise every time a car zooms by your window. Such stimuli are new to you, hence you react to them, disturbing your sleep. However, after about a month, these noises no longer disrupt your sleep; you have habituated.

Habituation is a form of learning where we become accustomed to new stimuli, eventually ceasing to react to them. Think of it as a form of memory. We stop reacting to certain stimuli because our experiences and memories of these stimuli inform us that they are not threatening or noteworthy. In other words, the stimuli have lost their novelty and no longer trigger the same reaction.

This behavioral adaptation occurs not just in humans, but in other species, too, even in human fetuses as young as 37–40 weeks. This form of learning facilitates our adaptation to new environments and reduces our sensitivity to repetitive, non-threatening stimuli.

The Flip Side of the Coin: Sensitization

Now, let's examine the opposite of habituation: sensitization. Instead of becoming less responsive to stimuli, we become more sensitive to them. Our reaction to a stimulus increases each time it's presented.

Imagine a dog sleeping on the floor. A loud bang outside the window makes it lift its head but stay put. Another bang occurs, and the dog raises its ears and looks worried. A third bang results in the dog standing up and whimpering. Each bang has made the dog increasingly alert, thereby sensitizing it.

Interestingly, sensitization is not specific to a stimulus. For instance, if our aforementioned dog hears a door slamming inside the house after the external bangs, it might react with fear even though it usually disregards such noise. The dog is on high alert due to prior experiences, enhancing its responses to all potential threats.

Implications

As we delve deeper into these phenomena, it's crucial to remember that habituation and sensitization occur regardless of whether they're beneficial or detrimental to us. We can get used to unpleasant or even dangerous environments, just as we can become overly sensitized to non-threatening stimuli.

While habituation helps us adapt to new environments and ignore the "noise" of unimportant stimuli, sensitization prepares us for potential dangers. As a social pedagogue, I believe it is crucial to understand these processes as they provide a better understanding of how we interact with our environment and the stimuli within it.

Remember, dear readers, the knowledge of these psychological concepts can greatly influence how we shape our lives, respond to our environment, and understand our emotional and physical reactions.

The Interplay Between Mindset and Money

Money, much like other aspects of life, isn't just a physical entity; it's a psychological construct deeply intertwined with our emotions, perceptions, and life experiences. Financial behaviors, often passed down through generations or formed by past experiences, can significantly impact our economic well-being and broader life quality.

I've often encountered the profound influences that past experiences can have on individuals' attitudes toward money. Drawing on the principles of social pedagogy — an approach that combines education and social work with a focus on holistic development — I intend to explore the relationship between mindset and money, shedding light on how past experiences shape financial behaviors.

In this article, I delve into the interplay between the mind and money, underscoring the importance of financial education, the role of emotional intelligence, and how a social pedagogical approach can foster healthier financial behaviors.

The Power of Mindset on Financial Decisions

Our mental schema — comprised of our beliefs, attitudes, and experiences — plays a crucial role in shaping our financial decisions. These schemas can be traced back to our childhood and are often influenced by our parents' financial habits and attitudes towards money.

While these schemas can serve as useful shortcuts, helping us navigate complex financial landscapes, they can also lead us down treacherous paths. For instance, a person raised in a household where money was constantly scarce may develop a scarcity mindset, leading them to overly cautious or risky financial behaviors. On the other hand, individuals who grow up in affluent households may develop a mindset of abundance, which could lead to unsustainable spending patterns or a disregard for the value of money.

The influence of these schemas extends beyond our personal lives — it can also shape societal and economic structures. It's here that the principles of social pedagogy come into play.

Social Pedagogy and Financial Education

Social pedagogy centers around fostering learning and development in a holistic and integrated manner. It believes in the transformative power of education — not just in the traditional academic sense, but in shaping attitudes, values, and behaviors.

In the context of financial behavior, social pedagogy underscores the importance of financial education. But this isn't about merely understanding the difference between stocks and bonds or learning how to budget. It's about helping individuals understand their financial schemas and how they influence their financial behaviors.

This involves exploring one's financial history and unpacking the experiences and emotions associated with money. It also includes understanding the societal and cultural influences on one's financial mindset and the role of emotional intelligence in making financial decisions.

From Awareness to Action: The Role of Emotional Intelligence

Financial decisions, at their core, are emotional decisions. Whether it's the thrill of making a risky investment or the anxiety associated with debt, our emotions are integral to how we handle money.

Emotional intelligence — our ability to understand, manage, and positively use our emotions — plays a crucial role in making sound financial decisions. It allows us to recognize and regulate our emotional responses to financial situations, preventing us from making impulsive decisions driven by fear, greed, or stress.

A social pedagogical approach to financial education includes fostering emotional intelligence. It's about helping individuals recognize the emotional triggers that lead to harmful financial behaviors and equipping them with the skills to manage these triggers effectively.

Final thoughts

Our relationship with money is complex and deeply personal, shaped by a myriad of factors from our past experiences to our emotional responses. As a social pedagogue, I believe in the transformative power of education, self-awareness, and emotional intelligence in shaping healthier financial behaviors.

We need to look beyond the numbers and understand the human side of money. By doing so, we can not only improve our financial well-being but also contribute to a more equitable and financially literate society.

Unveiling the Heart of Child Psychotherapy

I'd like to delve into an intricate and fascinating world where childhood, psychology, and therapy meet. In this arena, both intricate processes and unique encounters take place that are not always visible to the untrained eye. Welcome, as we explore this universe of child psychotherapy together, illuminating its core from a social pedagogical lens.

Historically, child psychotherapy has been considered a protected place, a refuge from the world where children can express themselves without the fear of exposure or judgment. However, this insularity can sometimes be unsatisfactory in clinical work, research, and broader social contexts. By making psychotherapy sessions less closed off to external insights, we can reduce the risk of ineffective or harmful practices and encourage understanding of effective change processes.

Child psychotherapy

Capturing the essence of child psychotherapy can be challenging due to its multifaceted nature. The therapy sessions are as unique as the individual encounters between children and psychotherapists. Multiple questions arise. What happens in the therapeutic encounter between the psychotherapist and the child? What is their interaction contributes to the evolution of psychotherapy? How does the psychotherapist act in the room compared to the prescribed techniques and theoretical basis? How can we understand occurrences that are universally human and are effective in all human meetings in relation to therapeutic processes?

In my journey as a social pedagogue working with children with NDD, my interest was piqued by the individual differences among psychotherapists. It became clear how psychotherapists could vary greatly within the same form of psychotherapy, and how the therapist's personal style could directly influence the therapy process. I also noted how much the meeting between patient and therapist was influenced by the patient's issues and personality, contributing to the unique character and course of each therapy.

The practice of successful therapy

The question of how processes develop in child psychotherapy has yet to be answered satisfactorily. However, the increasing use of video recordings of therapy sessions in recent years provides valuable insights into therapists' interactions with children, leading to new questions about how the therapeutic encounter evolves and facilitates change processes. Moreover, as child psychotherapy continues to evolve, the focus has shifted from studying verbal statements to non-verbal happenings, such as body language and the affective meeting between the child and the psychotherapist.

It's also essential to recognize that seeking help comes in different shapes and sizes. Some families may be driven to therapy out of concern from relatives or school health staff, while others may seek help with familiarity and hope. An inseparable part of the therapeutic encounter is how motivation and expectations are created and expressed by children, parents, and psychotherapists.

Final thoughts

The perception of childhood and children's mental health has changed over time, molded by sociocultural and historical contexts. How children are viewed directly impacts the therapeutic encounter. Children's experiences are shaped by adult views of childhood, opinions on the child's place in society, and interventions deemed necessary.

In conclusion, it's evident that child psychotherapy is not just a simple process but a dance between the child, the therapist, and societal expectations. As we continue to learn and grow in our understanding of this complex field, we must remember that every child is unique, and their therapy should be tailored to their individual needs. In the end, the goal is to create a safe, understanding space where children can express themselves and grow positively.

The Pursuit of Meaning: A Perspective on Existential Meaning in Life

Social pedagogy, a broad discipline that encompasses a myriad of perspectives, fundamentally underpins inclusion, the fostering of human learning, the potential for change, personal empowerment, and development (Molin & Bolin, 2018; Madsen, 2001). Through these foundational principles, it endeavors to illuminate individuals' opportunities and shape their life conditions (Hämäläinen, 2012). At its core, it seeks to encourage participation in meaningful contexts, emphasizing the critical relationship between the individual and society (Bolin & Molin, 2018; Madsen, 2001). However, it often risks overlooking societal shortcomings, instead focusing predominantly on the individual's deficiencies (Hämäläinen, 2012).

This article explores how people perceive existential meaning and how it correlates with the field of social pedagogy. We dive deep into the existential aspects of human needs and spiritual distress — elements that Payne (2015) asserts all humans encounter — with an aim to enrich the quality of life.

As a dedicated Social Pedagogue and a devout Protestant Christian belonging to Svenska Kyrkan, I often find that my professional and spiritual lives are inextricably linked. Faith and social pedagogy, in my view, share a substantial common ground.

In my profession, the principles of social pedagogy stress the importance of relationships and holistic education. It emphasizes empathy, respect, and understanding, which resonate profoundly with my Christian beliefs that preach love, acceptance, and charity. My work as a social pedagogue is an avenue for the practical application of these faith-based values, where I can foster a sense of belonging, community, and mutual respect among the people I work with.

My role as a mother of three sons further enriches this journey. Raising my children in the faith, they have grown into believers and individuals with a strong moral compass. Seeing them become good, kind, and respectful individuals, I feel a sense of fulfillment knowing that the values I have imparted, influenced by my faith and my profession, have guided them well.

Understanding and accepting spirituality's role in human life is paramount for comprehending numerous clients' needs and experiences. This understanding contributes to a balanced approach in social work, which is otherwise dominated by rationalist, secular, and evidence-based values. The absence of existential values in social work echoes in Broström's (2018) study on elder care, highlighting a "compact silence" regarding existential questions and existential anxiety.

Interestingly, the World Value Survey reveals that Sweden stands out among other countries. It's a country culturally and structurally defined by secular, rational, and individualistic values, highlighting the absence of an existential perspective.

I would like to bring my unique experiences from my background to highlight the significance of the existential perspective in social work. I have noticed a recurring focus on quantifiable aspects of a person's life. Yet, what about the immeasurable aspects of a person? Where do they find space?

Drawing from Frankl's (2006) theory, we define existential meaning as a fundamental existential condition for humans. By virtue of existing, humans have a will for meaning and aspire for a meaningful life.

Frankl (2006) emphasizes that the meaning of life is fluid, varying from person to person. However, we cannot grasp this meaning through intellect alone; it must be believed in, based on our whole being. Notwithstanding the inevitability of death, life isn't meaningless. Instead, we must confront our inability to rationally comprehend life's absolute meaningfulness. This underlines the role of love in human interaction, crucial to seeing possibilities in people (Frankl, 2006).

Our existence inevitably confronts us with our will to meaning, something that shouldn't be invented but discovered. This meaning must be found by the individual themselves for it to be significant. This understanding underscores the fundamental role of existential perspectives in social pedagogy, potentially catalyzing transformative change and development.

This blending of faith and social pedagogy brings a unique perspective to my life and work, allowing me to create a wholesome environment that nourishes not just the physical and intellectual needs of individuals, but also caters to their spiritual well-being.

The interconnectedness of these two vital aspects of my life demonstrates the profound impact they have on shaping our communities. Faith and social pedagogy, despite appearing as separate domains, can intertwine to enhance social cohesion, mutual respect, and the holistic development of individuals.

The Influence of Carl Rogers on Social Pedagogy

In my life, I've encountered various theories, strategies, and philosophies regarding child development, emotional intelligence, and human psychology. However, one particular theory that has resonated deeply with me and profoundly shaped my approach toward pedagogy is Carl Rogers' Humanistic Psychology. Also known as the silent revolution, Rogers' philosophy is a beacon of hope that illuminates our path as we navigate the intricate labyrinth of human potential.

Carl Rogers: The Silent Revolution

Carl Rogers' humanistic psychology, revered as the silent revolution, centralizes the person in the therapeutic process. It's all about empathizing with their stories and nurturing the growth of their potential. This humanistic approach emerged as a necessary shift in psychotherapy, challenging the passive and deterministic perspective often applied in psychoanalysis and behaviorism.

Rogers emphasized our ability to develop, construct a better world, and encouraged us to take responsibility for ourselves while being receptive to new experiences. He proposed non-directive therapy to assist individuals in enhancing their self-awareness.

A Revolution in Practice

After World War II, Rogers offered psychological assistance to soldiers returning home traumatized and physically wounded. Back then, these young men's care was limited to physical treatment, neglecting the equally pressing emotional trauma. Rogers' humanistic psychology aimed to simplify the healing process, addressing the need for emotional analysis and treatment.

In the wake of his successful psychological interventions, Japan invited Rogers to share his techniques with their psychologists. His revolutionary approach to therapy not only astonished the world but also led to his nomination for the Nobel Peace Prize.

Self-Improvement: The Heart of Rogers' Theory

Rogers' personal life mirrored the principles of his theory, focusing on self-improvement and exploring the elements that characterize us as we strive toward our goals. Interestingly, he began his career in agricultural science, later delving into Eastern and Western religions, then earning degrees in history and theology.

Eventually, he gravitated towards psychopedagogy, influenced by one of his personal heroes, John Dewey. From Dewey, Rogers learned that education is not only an intellectual experience but also an emotional journey. His humanistic psychology was soon recognized as a critical part of the humanist psychology movement, thanks to his client-centered therapy.

Exploring the Real 'You'

Rogers replaced the term 'patient' with 'client' in his therapy, putting them on the same level as the therapist, thereby challenging the traditional therapist-patient dynamic. He believed in the possibility of positive change, the breakdown of defense mechanisms, and the formation of an impetus toward self-improvement and goal attainment.

The primary goal of his therapy was not to provide solutions or strategies but to listen, facilitate the acknowledgment of feelings, and assist clients in defining their own personalities. His psychological focus remains one of our best strategies for handling trauma and personal dependencies, even today.

Final Thoughts: The Path Towards Personal Transformation

Rogers presents us with an ethos of self-awareness, self-acceptance, and transformation — an ethos that rings true to many a parent, teacher, and, indeed, social pedagogue.

By connecting deeply with our authentic selves and confronting both our positive and negative emotions, we create a roadmap for personal growth. It reminds us that every individual, child or adult, is more than just a passive receiver of information or help. Each of us possesses the capacity to be an active participant in our own lives, shaping our paths and reaching our potential.

Rogers's approach doesn't just resonate with me as a professional social pedagogue, but also as a mother to three wonderful sons. The Rogersian principles of empathy, authenticity, and growth are not only integral in my professional interactions but are also values I strive to impart to my children. It is through practicing these principles that we can effectively bridge the gaps between people, enabling them to understand and empathize with one another on a deeper level.

In essence, Rogers' humanistic psychology teaches us that personal development is not an unattainable ideal. On the contrary, it is a constant process, a journey of self-discovery and self-improvement, which we all have the power to embark on.

Just like Rogers' journey from agriculture to Eastern and Western religions, to history, theology, and eventually, psychology, we too are capable of significant self-growth and transformation. We are not bound by our past or present circumstances; we have the power to shape our future selves.

This transformative perspective is not only empowering but also unites us in the shared human experience of self-discovery and personal development. Whether we are a child in need of guidance, a parent nurturing their young, or a social pedagogues reaching out to others, we are all on this journey of becoming the best version of ourselves.

It's this intersection of personal and professional growth where Rogers' principles really shine, serving as a beacon for all those navigating the complex seas of life. The essence of his teachings — a deeply held respect for the individual's capacity for self-actualization — is the underpinning of my work and the way I live my life. The principles of humanistic psychology continue to guide my path, both as a mother and a social pedagogue, enabling me to foster authentic, empathetic relationships with those around me.

Blending Pedagogical Psychology, Parenting, and The Power of Connection

In my life I wear multiple hats. My roles intertwine, enriching each other, and fueling my passion to share and learn from everyone around me. Together, we will delve into the heart of pedagogical psychology, understanding how we learn and how we teach.

Pedagogical psychology is a fascinating field dedicated to exploring the processes of teaching and learning. It seeks answers to critical questions like, "How do we learn?" and "How can we teach better?" The discipline's principles have shaped my career as a social pedagogue and my life as a parent, helping me guide my sons and my students on their unique learning journeys.

The wonderful Chinese proverb reminds us, "Learning is a treasure that will follow its owner everywhere." And I can't agree more! In this article, we will uncover the fundamentals of pedagogical psychology, explore its primary models, and understand its practical application in real-world settings.

The Birth of Pedagogical Psychology

Before we delve into the specifics of pedagogical psychology, let's take a brief tour of its origins. Coll, one of the authors who first approached pedagogical psychology in 1990, made two key discoveries:

1. Pedagogical psychology relates to the application of psychology's principles to pedagogical theory and practice.
2. There's disagreement on almost everything else, including

what the application comprises, the content it covers, and its relationship with other areas within psychology.

One of the defining challenges for pedagogical psychology has been its lack of identity. It's born out of the intersection between psychology and education, with varying opinions among specialties regarding whether it's basic or applied knowledge. Despite this, pedagogical psychology has progressively defined itself and solidified into a robust discipline within the psychological and educational realm.

Defining Pedagogical Psychology

Today, pedagogical psychology can be defined as the branch of psychology responsible for studying change processes that occur in individuals due to their relationships with formal or informal educational institutions such as schools or families. It differs from psychopedagogy, which focuses on studying the psychological processes involved in learning and teaching throughout life.

Pedagogical psychology also examines human learning patterns and teaching methods. One of its key objectives is to analyze the effectiveness of educational interventions. Ultimately, it aims to enhance different interventions, studying how people learn and focusing its attention on subgroups of students, including highly able children or those with disabilities.

As Ignacio Estrada rightly said, "If a child cannot learn the way we teach, maybe we should teach in the way they learn." This is where the true essence of pedagogical psychology lies: adapting to the learner's needs rather than forcing them to adapt to the teaching method.

Theories of Pedagogical Psychology

Pedagogical psychology encompasses various theories and models. Among the most significant ones are the behavioral and cognitive models, including the classical conditioning model by Watson, the instrumental conditioning model by Thorndike, Skinner's operant conditioning model, and the cognitive models by Bandura, Information Processing (IP), and Gagné.

These models have practical applications in education and child psychology. Pedagogical psychologists often work in schools, private practices, and special education centers. They assist students with special educational needs, understanding that these students learn better when knowledge is delivered in a way that deviates from the norm for their age.

Final Thoughts

Pedagogical psychology resides at the intersection of psychology and education, providing insights into how we learn from a young age. It is from this foundation of understanding that I, as a social pedagogue and mother, continue to engage, learn, and guide the learning journeys of my sons and my students.

Together, let's continue to explore, grow, and celebrate the power of learning. After all, learning is a treasure, accompanying us throughout our lives, empowering us, and fostering meaningful connections along the way.

An Intercultural Approach in Swedish Education

I have a deeply personal journey that I want to share with you. I am a firm believer that every story is unique, with the potential to inspire change. The story I am about to share today is about embracing diversity at the heart of Swedish Education.

Swedish Education

Sweden is a nation that is home to more than 200 different cultures, making it a vibrant, multicultural society. Two million of Sweden's nine million inhabitants represent these diverse cultures, a conscious policy choice that sets Sweden apart from many European countries where only two or three cultures are typically represented (Lorentz, 2007). In light of this richness, it becomes important to examine how education, a cornerstone of any society, is addressing this diversity.

In Sweden, both the compulsory education curriculum (Skolverket, 2006a) and the preschool curriculum (Skolverket, 2006b) state that school is a social and cultural meeting place. With increasing mobility across national borders, diversity in preschool and school grows, creating an environment where students can gain awareness of their own culture and actively participate in the common cultural heritage. This multi-cultural context raises some questions: How does work in multi-cultural children's groups and preschool classes function? Do educators see children's cultural backgrounds as an asset? How do educators work with children's cultural backgrounds in their practice? And, is this work based on an intercultural approach?

Cultural background

Cultural background is not just language, our most significant cultural heritage, but so much more. It encompasses three dimensions — the material, visible through products of craftsmanship and technology; the mental, which covers knowledge, attitudes, beliefs, and values; and the social, which incorporates fixed relationships between people and how we interact with each other (Jernström & Johansson, 1997). When educators meet a group of children, they meet as many cultures as there are children, regardless of whether the children have different national backgrounds or not.

Understanding culture in this broader sense is important for a couple of reasons. First, it allows us to treat all children with the respect and dignity they deserve. Secondly, it encourages a sense of inclusivity among students and creates an environment where all students feel valued and accepted. The "intercultural approach" to education is one way to achieve this. It's the process where people of different languages and cultures communicate with each other, seeing each other's cultures as assets, not liabilities. It requires educators to continuously reflect on their beliefs and values regarding cultural and linguistic differences and strive to develop an intercultural approach (Skolverket, 2005).

Monolingual, multicultural and intercultural

Let's discuss the terms monolingual, multicultural, and intercultural. Monocultural means that "Swedishness" is the norm. Multicultural means increasing understanding for students with immigrant backgrounds and minorities. Intercultural implies that all children get to express themselves and communicate with each other, sharing their unique cultural backgrounds (Spowe, 2007).

While acknowledging diversity is important, it is equally critical to respect and promote cultural differences. In Benhabib's words, we often hear that it's good to preserve and strive for such cultures and cultural differences (Benhabib, 2004).

Final thoughts

The multicultural society I live in and the multicultural classrooms I work in, enrich me both as an individual and as a professional. Being a mother to three boys, I am aware of the importance of instilling respect and appreciation for cultural diversity in my children. The Swedish educational system is built upon the understanding that every child's language and cultural background are vital. By applying this understanding, as well as the principles of social pedagogy, I work to empower children to explore their identities, languages, and cultures in a safe and inclusive environment.

In conclusion, the multicultural makeup of Sweden's population is not just a demographic fact; it's an invaluable resource. As a Social Pedagogue, mother, and citizen, I am proud to play a part in fostering the intercultural approach in education and nurturing a future generation that not only accepts diversity but thrives in it.

Fostering Media Literacy in Children

I would like to share with you my thoughts and experiences on how media impacts children's lives and the crucial role that education plays in enabling them to navigate this ever-evolving landscape effectively.

Children and Media: A World of Impressions

The world that our children live in today is saturated with a constant flow of information. As the famous Swedish pedagogue, Birgitta Olsson, who works as a film pedagogue in Kungsbacka, Sweden, suggests, this rapid stream of impressions is a world in which our children must learn to orientate, create context, sort, and evolve. It's increasingly complex for us to interpret and relate to media representations of our contemporary life and history.

One truth Birgitta highlighted is the reality that there's more than one truth in the world, making it crucial to understand media language and influence. Living in a media-influenced existence, children are exposed to various aspects of life long before they encounter them personally and gain their experiences. This scenario introduces the concept of the film narrative as raw material that readily fascinates children. A powerful film experience can start a process that invites conversation, reflection, and knowledge-seeking, creating a multitude of alternative models, thought processes, patterns, and lifestyles.

Media in Children's Lives: A Double-Edged Sword

But where does the responsibility lie for children's awareness and knowledge about the media? Birgitta posits that schools play a significant role in this process. If schools aren't prepared to provide space for reflection and understanding, we risk media literacy segregation, which limits our life choices and distances us from equality and democracy [1].

According to Mary Megee, Principal at the Media Education Laboratory at Rutgers University Network College of Arts and Science, children's understanding of the world can be profoundly affected by media. If they cannot handle and interpret information and media, it is easy for them to take everything they see as the truth and the prevailing norm. Over time, this unquestioning acceptance often leads to cynicism — from believing everything to believing nothing the media conveys.

However, it's important to distinguish between cynicism and skepticism. Being skeptical involves questioning, judging, distinguishing differences, and recognizing motives. The ability to critically analyze the information we receive is a key aspect of media literacy.

Critical Thinking: A Key Tool for Media Literacy

Crucial in this regard are skills such as discerning facts from value judgments, assessing source credibility, evaluating the truth of a statement, separating relevant from irrelevant information, recognizing bias, and identifying undisclosed assumptions. These skills, however, do not develop in a vacuum and require a certain level of guidance and training from educators.

For critical reflection to occur, the subject matter must be meaningful to the student. Pedagogue Ann-Britt Enochsson, who works at Karlstad University, has studied how fourth-grade students interact with internet searches. Her research suggests that the more the students learned about the internet and the more complex their perception of the internet became, the more willing they were to reflect on the credibility of the content and see the meaningfulness in doing so.

The Role of Critical Reflection in Learning

Louise Limberg, a professor at the Library School in Borås, emphasizes the significance of critical thinking in learning. Her study exploring the interplay between information search and learning shows that the amount of time students spent on analysis, interpretation, and critical thinking was crucial in understanding a subject holistically and, in turn, achieving better learning results.

Therefore, the development of critical thinking and a holistic perspective in relation to information and media is not only important for children's media consumption but also crucial for knowledge retention.

However, schools and their staff, while mandated to follow the school law and curriculum, often lack specific directives on how these goals should be achieved. It is up to us, educators, parents, and guardians, to bridge this gap and provide meaningful media education to our children.

We are in an era where media literacy is not just an option; it's a necessity. Our children's future in this ever-connected world depends on it. Let's take this journey together and make a difference.

The Cognitive Perspective in Child Development and Education

As a social pedagogue, I work daily with children, helping them navigate their personal and academic worlds. As a mother of three sons, I have witnessed firsthand the profound effect that our beliefs and thought processes have on our behavior, emotions, and overall development. In today's post, I want to delve into the fascinating world of the cognitive perspective, a pillar in psychology that shapes our understanding of children's behavior.

The Cognitive Perspective: A Decoding Tool

Established in the mid-20th century, the cognitive perspective has its roots in the idea that our thoughts govern our emotions and behaviors. These thoughts exist within mental schemas, developed from our past experiences. From these experiences, we also create foundational beliefs about ourselves. Such beliefs may range from positive affirmations like "I am good enough as I am" to negative thoughts like "I am worthless". These foundational beliefs influence how we interpret situations.

Imagine two children witnessing a group of whispering peers. One child with a negative foundational belief about herself may interpret the whispers as being about her, causing feelings of discomfort. The other child, with a positive foundational belief, may simply assume the group is sharing confidences, thus not evoking any emotional response.

Psychological conservatism, another concept in the cognitive perspective, further explains why a person with a negative foundational belief tends to interpret situations negatively. This tendency validates their belief, turning it into a self-fulfilling prophecy.

The ABC Model

Albert Ellis, a renowned psychologist, developed the ABC model to illustrate how thoughts, feelings, and behaviors are interconnected:

- A for Activating Event
- B for Beliefs, Thoughts, Assumptions
- C for Emotional Consequences

Events we experience (A) are processed in our brains, which weave in past experiences and foundational beliefs (B), thus triggering an emotional response (C).

Learned Helplessness

In the 1970s, psychologist Martin Seligman introduced the concept of learned helplessness. According to Seligman, there are two thought styles concerning whether we can influence our situation. One style believes that occurrences depend on external factors or others, whereas the other style believes in self-accountability, allowing for changing situations.

Aaron Beck and Depression

Aaron Beck developed a cognitive theory to explain depression, emphasizing three types of thinking central to the depressed:

1. Negative Self-Image (Negative Foundational Belief)
2. A Negative View of Experiences
3. A Negative Outlook on the Future

Emphasizing Psychological Evaluations in Schools

Since the new school law was enacted in 2010 in Sweden, access to psychologists became a statutory initiative in student health. Children, as individuals, have a right to be met with respect and understanding in school, with their learning and development conditions tailored to their needs.

In cases where adjustments in the environment or pedagogy do not yield the desired results, it may be necessary to investigate individual factors in the child. As a social pedagogue, my role is to understand the child better and ensure that any evaluation or intervention benefits the child.

Final Thoughts

Understanding the cognitive perspectives and implementing the associated strategies are crucial steps towards achieving effective social pedagogy. By recognizing the importance of these perspectives in shaping children's behavior, we can open new possibilities for intervention and facilitate constructive change.

Being a social pedagogue and a mother, I've experienced first-hand how these perspectives guide the way our children perceive themselves and the world around them. From a simple classroom interaction to a child's response to life's adversities, cognitive perspectives are at the core. They provide the framework through which children interpret and understand their experiences, shaping their emotional responses and behaviors.

Every child's journey through life is different, as are their cognitive schemas. Our job, as social pedagogues and parents, is to help children realize their potential by enabling them to challenge negative beliefs and replace them with positive self-perceptions. When we succeed in doing this, we create an environment where children can thrive and develop resilience, no matter what life throws at them.

As we navigate the challenges of our own lives, let us remember the power of cognitive perspectives. They not only explain our behavior but also offer a beacon of hope in our quest to help children develop a healthy perception of self. It is not an easy task, but with dedication, empathy, and understanding, we can guide our children towards a future where they recognize their worth and potential.

Lastly, let us not forget the vital role that education plays in this mission. Schools, through their curriculum and psychological services, can be a powerful ally in our efforts. It is not only about achieving good grades or excelling in a particular subject but also about fostering an environment that recognizes and respects each child's unique perspective and journey.

So, let's keep the conversation going. Let's continue to learn, adapt, and grow, not just for ourselves but also for our children. And remember, your efforts in understanding and applying cognitive perspectives in social pedagogy are more than just a professional obligation — they are a personal commitment to making a positive difference in the lives of children.

Bridging the Gap through Communication and Leadership

I've spent years studying, understanding, and applying the principles of pedagogy in my personal and professional life. Rooted deeply in psychology, sociology, and philosophy, pedagogy has evolved its unique identity as a socio-humanistic discipline that encompasses the multifaceted learning and development journey of humans, enriched by the communication and interaction that happens in our daily encounters.

Pedagogy highlights the significant aspects of nurturing, teaching, and educating from an individual, societal, cultural, and broader social perspective. This discipline majorly extracts knowledge from two fields: pedagogical psychology and pedagogical sociology, which form the foundations of the learning I impart in my role as a social pedagogue.

Pedagogical psychology delves into the psychological aspects of learning and development processes. It revolves around theories of how humans learn and develop, both individually and socially, and how they are socialized into different contexts. It aims to understand how various pedagogical situations and learning environments impact learning, creating tools to help us empathize with various pedagogical situations and stimulate and support people's learning and development in different contexts.

On the other hand, pedagogical sociology encompasses knowledge about humans' upbringing and the various conditions for development and learning, taking a more overarching societal perspective on upbringing, teaching, and education. It explores how individuals participate in, are shaped by, and shape their societies, cultures, and identities. This branch also studies pedagogical institutions and organizations such as families, schools, workplaces, and recreational activities, and their roles in society. Factors such as societal changes, gender, social, cultural, and ethnic backgrounds, and various disabilities are known to influence this.

In my work, I've observed that communication holds the key to effective pedagogy. The concept of communication, linked closely to the subject of pedagogy and social psychology, centers on human interactions from a group and leadership perspective. It is often the glue that holds all elements of pedagogy together.

One integral part of pedagogy is leadership, especially "pedagogical leadership," which involves leveraging knowledge about human interaction and communication and the social context's importance, relating it to leadership. It also revolves around leadership's role in fostering people's learning and growth.

This intricate dance of pedagogy is particularly critical when communicating with individuals with underdeveloped skills, who may have difficulty understanding contexts or interpreting things literally. Misunderstandings can easily occur, leading to conflicts and problem behaviors. Thus, it is crucial to reflect on what we say, how we say it, and whether we mean what we say.

Our communication is both verbal and non-verbal, involving more than spoken words. Tone, gestures, facial expressions, glances, and the unspoken — things said between the lines, not stated outright but implied by the context — all play a part.

We all possess varying communication skills, and stress can reduce our ability to receive, process, and reciprocate information. Individuals with developmental variations, such as autism, often have limited communication abilities and are sensitive to stress. Hence, those of us working with individuals with such conditions need to be mindful of our communication style and maintain a stress-free environment to be as calm and clear as possible, and to avoid transmitting stress.

In my journey as a social pedagogue, every day is a new learning experience — a chance to bridge the gap between individuals, lead with empathy and understanding, and navigate the complex interplay of pedagogy, psychology, and sociology for better societal integration.

About the Author

Katherine Myrestad is a passionate social pedagogue, dedicated writer, and loving single mother to three sons. With a life richly woven through the threads of care, education, and spiritual coaching, she brings a unique and nurturing perspective to the world of child education and development. Her journey through motherhood, coupled with her professional endeavors, has gifted her with profound insights into the delicate art of shaping young minds.

Read more at https://linktr.ee/vanirheim.